FORMATION

OF THE

CHRISTIAN CHARACTER

FORMATION

OF THE

CHRISTIAN CHARACTER,

ADDRESSED TO THOSE WHO ARE SEEKING TO LEAD A RELIGIOUS LIFE:

AND

PROGRESS OF THE CHRISTIAN LIFE;

BEING

A SEQUEL TO THE "FORMATION OF THE CHRISTIAN CHARACTER."

BY HENRY WARE, JR.

NEW EDITION.

BOSTON:
AMERICAN UNITARIAN ASSOCIATION.
1874.

PREFACE.

In presenting to the religious public this little book, the writer has only to say, that he undertook it because he thought that a work of this character was needed and would be welcome. During his active ministry, he had often felt the want of a book on personal religion, different, in some respects, from any which had fallen in his way; and when compelled by ill health to relinquish his pastoral cares, he attempted to beguile some of the languid hours of a weary convalescence by efforts at composing such an one. The result has come very far short of the idea which he had formed in his mind. The book was written at distant and uncertain intervals, upon journeys and in public houses, and has been now revised for the press in the midst of other cares, which have allowed no time for giving it the completeness he desired. Yet, as it belongs to a class of writings of whose importance he has the highest sense, and the multiplication of which, as well as the increase of a taste for their perusal, he esteems in the highest measure desirable,—he ventures to hope that this slight effort will not be wholly lost; and that it may at least do something towards exciting others to a preparation of more efficient works, which shall nourish the spirit of devotion, and extend the power of practical faith.

Cambridge, May 16, 1831.

CONTENTS.

FORMATION

OF THE

CHRISTIAN CHARACTER.

INTRODUCTION.

I AM anxious to bespeak the reader's right attention before he enters on the following pages. They have been written only for those who are sincerely desirous of knowing themselves, and are bent upon forming a re- igious character. They can be of little nterest or value to any other person, or if read with any other view than that of self-improvement. I venture therefore to entreat every one, into whose hands the book may fall, to peruse it, as it has been written, not for entertainment, but for moral edification; to read it at those seasons when he is seriously disposed, and can reflect upon the important topics presented to his view. I am solicitous to aid him in the formation of his Christian character, and about every other result I am indifferent.

I would even presume, further, to warn one class of readers, and that not a small one, against a danger which lurks even in their established respect for religion. That general regard for it, which grows out of the circumstances of education and the habits of society, may be mistaken for a religious state of mind; yet it is perfectly consistent with religious indifference. A man may sincerely honor, advocate, and uphold the religion of Christ on account of its general influence, its beneficial public tendency, its humane and civilizing consequences, without at all subjecting his own temper and life to its laws, or being in any proper sense a subject of the peculiar happiness it imparts. This is perhaps not an infrequent case. Men need to be made sensible that religion is a personal thing, a matter of personal application and experience. Unless it is so considered, it will scarcely be an object of earnest pursuit, or of fervent, hearty interest, nor can it exert its true and thorough influence on the character. Indeed, its desirable influence upon the state of society can be gained only through this deep personal devotion to it of individuals; because none but this is genuine religion, and the genuine only can exhibit the genuine power.

I know of nothing to be more earnestly desired, than that men should cease to look upon religion as designed for others, and should come to regard it as primarily affecting themselves; that they should first and most seriously study its relation to their own hearts, and be above all things anxious about their own characters. His is but a partial and unsatisfactory faith, which is concerned wholly with the state of society in general, and allows him to neglect the discipline of his own affections and the culture of his own spiritual nature. He is but poorly fitted to honor or promote the cause of Christ, who has not first subjected his own soul to his holy government. There are men enough, when Christianity is prevalent and honorable, to lend it their countenance and pay it external homage. We want more thorough, consistent exemplifications of its purity, benevolence, and spirituality. These can be found only in men, who love it for its own sake, and because it is 'the wisdom of God and the power of God unto salvation,' and not simply because it is respectable in the eyes of the world, and favorable to the decency and order of the commonwealth. It is for those who are seeking this end, and for such only, that I write.

CHAPTER I.

THE NATURE OF RELIGION, AND WHAT WE ARE TO SEEK.

In order to the intelligent and successful pursuit of any object, it is necessary, first of all, to have a definite conception of what we desire to effect or obtain. This is especially important in the study of Religion, both because of the extent and variety of the subject itself, and because of the very different apprehensions of men respecting it. Many are disheartened and fail, in consequence of setting out with wrong views and false expectations. From which cause religion itself suffers; being made answerable for failures, which are entirely owing to the unreasonable anticipations and ill-directed efforts of those who enlisted in her service, but did not persevere in it.

Let us begin, then, with considering what is the object at which we aim when we seek a religious character.

Religion, in a general sense, is founded on man's relation and accountableness to his Maker: and it consists in cherishing the sentiments and performing the duties which thence result, and which belong to the other relations to other beings which God has appointed him to sustain.

Concerning these relations, sentiments, and duties, we are instructed in the Scriptures, especially in the New Testament. Religion, with us, is the *Christian* religion. It is found in the teachings and example of Jesus Christ It consists in the worship, the sentiments, and the character. which he enjoined, and which he illustrated in his own person.

What you are to seek, therefore, is, under the guidance of Jesus Christ, to feel your relation to God, and to live under a sense of responsibility to him; to cultivate assiduously those sentiments and affections which spring out of this responsible and filial relation, as well as those which arise out of your connexion with other men as his offspring; to perform all the duties to Him and them, which appertain to this character and relation; and to cherish that heavenward tendency of mind, which should spring from a consciousness of possessing an immortal nature. He who does all this is a religious man, or, in other words, a Christian.

You desire to be a Christian. To this are requisite three things: belief in the truths which the gospel reveals; possession of the state of mind which it enjoins; and performance of the duties which it requires: or, I may say, the subjection of the mind by faith, the subjection of the heart by love, the subjection of the will by obedience. This universal submission of yourself to God is what you are to aim at. This is Religion.

Observe how extensive a thing it is. It is a principle of the mind; founded upon thought, reflection, inquiry, argument; and leading to devotion and duty as most reasonable and suitable for intelligent beings.

It is a sentiment or affection of the heart; not the cold judgment of the intellect alone, in favor of what is right; but a warm, glowing feeling of preference and desire; a feeling, which attaches itself in love to the Father of all and to all good beings; which turns duty into inclination, and pursues virtue from impulse; which prefers and delights in that which is well pleasing to God, and takes an affectionate interest in the things to which the Saviour devoted himself.

It is a rule of life; it is the law of God; causing the external conduct to correspond to the principle which is established, and the sentiment which breathes, within; bringing every action into a conformity with the divine will, and making universal holiness the standard of the character.

The Scriptures represent religion under each of these different views. As a *principle*, it is called Faith; and in this view is Faith extolled as the essential thing for life and salvation. We are to 'walk by faith.' We are 'saved by faith.'—As a *sentiment*, it is styled Love. Love to God and man is declared by the Saviour to be the substance of religion; and the Apostles, especially John and Paul, every where represent this universal affection as the essence and the beauty of the Christian character. No one can read their language, and compare with it the life of Christ, without perceiving how essentially true religion is a sentiment of the heart.—As a *law* or *rule*, it is spoken of throughout the Scriptures. It is a commandment of God, requiring obedience. We are 'to do his will.' Christ is the 'author of salvation to those that obey him.' 'If thou wilt enter into life, keep the commandments.' 'He who keepeth my commandments, he it is that loveth me.'

In the general complexion of Scripture, and in many particular passages, these several views are united: thus we are told, that 'the fruit of the spirit is love, joy, peace, long-suffering, gentleness, goodness, faith, meekness, temperance;' that the blessing of God belongs to the humble, penitent, meek, pure in heart, merciful, and peaceful; that the Christian character consists in 'whatsoever is true, honest, just, pure, lovely, and of good report;' in adding to 'faith, virtue, knowledge, temperance, patience, godliness, brotherly kindness, and charity;' and 'in denying ungodliness and wordly lusts, and living soberly, righteously, and godly.'*

You see, then, what is the character of the

* Gal. v. 22, 23.—Matthew, v. 3–9.—Philip. iv. 8. -2 Peter, i. 6, 7—Titus, ii. 12.

religion which you are seeking. You perceive that it implies the absolute supremacy of the soul and its interests over all the objects and interests of the present state; and that its primary characteristic is a certain state of mind and affections. It is not the external conduct, not the observance of the moral law alone, which constitutes a religious man; but the principles from which he acts, the motives by which he is governed, the state of his heart. A principle of spiritual life pervades his intellectual nature, gives a complexion to his whole temper, and is the spring of that moral worth, which is in other men the result of education, circumstances, or interest. He is actuated by a prevailing sense of God, and the desire of a growing resemblance to his moral image. He is possessed with the perpetual consciousness of his immortality; and is not ashamed to deny himself any of the gratifications of the present hour, when thereby he may keep his mind more disengaged for the study of truth and the contemplation of his highest good. Living thus with his chief sources of happiness *within* him, he bears with equanimity the changes and trials of earth, and tastes something of the peculiar felicity of heaven, which is 'righteousness, and peace, and joy in a holy spirit;' and, like his master, who sojourned below, but whose affections were above, he does his Father's will as he passes through the world, but has treasured up his supreme good in his Father's future presence.

But if you would discern the full excellence and loveliness of the religious life, do not rest satisfied with studying the law, or musing over the descriptions of it. Go to the perfect pattern, which has been set before the believer for his guidance and encouragement. Look unto Jesus, the author and finisher of your faith. In him are exhibited all the virtues which you are to practise, all the affections and graces which you are to cultivate. In him is that rich assemblage of beautiful and attractive excellences, which has been the admiration of all reflecting men, the astonishment and eulogy of eloquent unbelievers, and the guide, consolation, and trust, of faithful disciples. In the dignity and sweetness which characterize him, how strongly do we feel that there is much more than a display of external qualities, conformity to a prescribed rule, and graceful propriety of outward demeanor. Nothing is more striking than the evident connexion of every thing which he said and did with something internal. The sentiment and disposition which reign within, are constantly visible through his exterior deportment; and we regard his words and his deeds less as distinct outward things, than as expressions or representations of character. As, in looking on certain countenances, we have no thought of color, feature, or form, but simply of the moral or intellectual qualities which they suggest; so, in contemplating the life of Jesus, we find ourselves perpetually looking beyond his mere actions, and fixing our thoughts on the qualities which they indicate. His life is but the expressive countenance of his soul. We feel, that, though in the midst of present things, he is led by principles, wrapt in thoughts, pervaded by sentiments, which are above earth, unearthly; that he is walking in communion with another sphere; and that the objects around him are matters of interest to him, no further than as they afford materials for the exercise of his benevolence, and opportunities for doing his Fa ther's will.

This is the personification of religion. This is the model which you are to imitate. And it is when you shall be imbued with this spirit, when you shall be filled with this sentiment, when your words, actions, and life, shall be only the spontaneous expression of this state of mind,—it is then that you will have attained the religious character, and become spiritually the child of God. You will have built up the kingdom of God within you; its purity, its devotion, and its peace, will be shed abroad in your heart, and thence will display themselves in the manners and conduct of your life.

To attain and perfect this character is to be the object of your desire, and the business of your life. You must never lose sight of it. In all that you learn, think, feel, and do, you are to have reference to this end. Whatever tends to promote this, you are to cherish and favor. Whatever hinders this, or in any degree operates injuriously upon it, you are to discountenance and shun. All

2

that gives bias to your passions and appetites, to your inclinations and thoughts, to your opinion of yourself, to your conduct toward others, your private or public employment of your time, your business and gains, your recreation and pleasures, is to be judged of by this standard, and condemned or approved accordingly. You are to feel that nothing is of such consequence to you as the Christian character; that to form this is the very work for which you were sent into the world; that if this be not done, you do nothing,—you had better never have been born; for your life is wasted without effecting its object, and your soul enters eternity without having secured its salvation. The provisions of God's mercy are slighted, and, for you, the Saviour has lived and died in vain.

It is plain, then, that the work to which you address yourself is arduous as well as delightful. It is not to be done in a short time, nor by a few indolent or violent efforts; not by an exercise of speculative reason, nor by an excitement of feeling, nor by assent to professions, forms, and rites; not by a love of hearing the word preached, nor by attention to the morals of ordinary life, nor by steadfastness in the virtues which are easy and pleasant;—but only by a surrender of the whole man and the entire life to the will of God, in faith, affection, and action; by a thorough imitation of Jesus in the devout and humble temper of his mind, in the spirituality of his affections, and in the purity and loveliness of his conduct. Any thing less than this, any partial, external, superficial conformity to a rule of decent living or ritual observance, must be wholly insufficient. For it cannot mould and rule the character, cannot answer the claims of the Creator upon his creatures, cannot prepare for the happiness which Jesus has revealed; a happiness so described, and so constituted, that none can be fitted for it, or be capable of enjoying it, but those who are earnestly and entirely conformed to the divine will. Who can relish the spiritual pleasures of eternity, that has not become spiritually minded? Who could enjoy admission to the society of Jesus and the spirits of the just made perfect, that is not like them? Why should one hope for heaven, and how expect to be happy there, if he have not formed a taste for its habits of purity, worship, and love?

Be on your guard, therefore, from the first, against setting your mark too low. Do not allow yourself to be persuaded that any thing less is Religion, or will answer for you, than its complete and highest measure. Remember that these things must be 'in you and abound.' The higher you aim, the higher you will reach; but if content with a low aim, you will forever fall short. The scriptural word is *Perfection.* Strive after that. Never be satisfied while short of it, and then you will be always improving. But if you set yourself some definite measure of goodness, if you prescribe to yourself some limit in devotion and love, you will by and by fancy you have reached it, and thus will remain stationary in a condition far below what you might have attained. Remember always, that you are capable of being more devout, more charitable, more humble, more devoted and earnest in doing good, better acquainted with religious truth; and that, as it is impossible there should be any period to the progress of the human soul, so it is impossible that the endeavor of the soul should be too exalted. It is because men do not think of this, or do not practically apply it, that so many, even of those who intend to govern themselves by religious motives, remain so lamentably deficient in excellence. They adopt a low or a partial standard, and strive after it sluggishly, and thus come to a period in religion before they arrive at the close of life. Happy they who are so filled with longings after spiritual good, that they go on improving to the end of their days.

CHAPTER II.

OUR POWER TO OBTAIN THAT WHICH WE SEEK.

The account which has been given of religion in the preceding chapter, shows it to be consonant to man's nature, and suited to the faculties with which God has endowed him. His soul is formed for religion, and the gospel has been adapted to the constitution of his soul. His understanding takes cognizance of its truths, his conscience applies them, his affections are capable of becoming interested in them, and his will of being subject to them. There can be no moment of existence, after he has come to the exercise of his rational faculties, at which this is not the case. As soon as he can love and obey his parents, he can love and obey God; and this is religion. The capacity of doing the one is the capacity of doing the other.

It is true, the latter is not so universally done as the former; but the cause is not, that religion is unsuited to the young, but that their attention is engrossed by visible objects and present pleasures. Occupied with these, it requires effort and pains-taking to direct the mind to invisible things; to turn the attention from the objects which press them on every side, to the abstract, spiritual objects of faith. Hence it is easy to see, that the want of early religion is owing, primarily, to the circumstances in which childhood is placed, and, next, to remissness in education Worldly things are before the child's eye, and minister to its gratification every hour and every minute; but religious things are presented to it only in a formal and dry way once a week. The things of the world are made to constitute its pleasures; those of religion are made its tasks. It is made to feel its dependence on a parent's love every hour; but is seldom reminded of its dependence on God, and then perhaps only in some stated lesson, which it learns by compulsion, and not in the midst of the actual engagements and pleasures of its little life. It partakes of the caresses of its human parents, and cannot remember the time when it was not an object of their tenderness; so that their image is interwoven with its very existence. But God it has never seen, and has seldom heard of him; his name and presence are banished from common conversation, and inferior and visible agents receive the gratitude for gifts which come from him. So also the parent's authority is immediate and visibly exercised, and obedience grows into the rule and habit of life. But the authority of God is not displayed in any sensible act or declaration; it is only heard of at set times and in set tasks; and thus it fails of becoming mingled with the principles of conduct, or forming a rule and habit of subjection.—In a word, let it be considered how little and how infrequently the idea of God is brought home to the child's mind, even under the most favorable circumstances, and how little is done to make him the object of love and obedience, in comparison with what is done to unite its affections to its parents; while, at the same time, the spirituality and invisibility of the Creator render it necessary that even more should be done;—and it will be seen that the want of an early and spontaneous growth of the religious character is not owing to the want of original capacity for religion, but is to be traced to the unpropitious circumstances in which childhood is passed, and the want of uniform, earnest, persevering instruction.

I have made this statement for two reasons. First, because I think it points out the immense importance of a religious education, and is an urgent call upon parents for greater diligence in this duty. No parent will deliberately say, in excuse for his neglect, that his children are incapable of apprehending and performing their duty to God. He will perceive that the same operation of circumstances and of unceasing influences, which has made them devoted to him, would make them devoted to God; and religion is that state of mind toward God, which a good child exercises toward a parent. It is the same principle and the same affections, fixing themselves on an infinitely higher object. Let parents be aware of this, and they will feel the call and the encouragement to a more systematic and affectionate attention to the religious instruction of their children.

I have made this statement, moreover, because it offers a guide to those who have passed through childhood without permanent religious impressions, and are now desirous of attaining them. It is principally for such that I write. They may be divided into many classes; some more and some less distant from the kingdom of God; some profligate, some indifferent; some with much goodness of outward performance, but with no internal principle of faith and piety; and some without even external conformity to right. But however differing in their past course of life, and in the peculiar habits and dispositions which characterize them, in one thing they now agree,—they are sensible of their errors and sins, and desire to apply themselves to that true and living way, which shall lead them to the favor of God and everlasting life. They feel that there is a great work to be done, a great change to be effected, either internally or externally, or both, and they are desirous to learn in what manner it shall be accomplished.

To such persons the statement which I have made above may be useful. Let them look back to it, and reflect upon it. God has given them powers for doing the work which he has assigned to them. That work is expressed in one word—the comprehensive name *Religion*. That work they should have begun and perseveringly pursued from their earliest days. But they have done otherwise. They have wandered from duty, and been unfaithful to God. They have gone far from him, like the unwise prodigal, and wasted the portion he gave them in vicious or unprofitable pursuits. They have cultivated the animal life; they have lived 'according to the flesh.' They need to cultivate the spiritual life; to live 'according to the spirit.' There is an animal life, and there is a spiritual life. Man is born into the first at the birth of his body; he is born into the second when he subjects himself to the power of religion, and prefers his rational and immortal to his sensual nature. During his earliest days, he is an animal only, pursuing, like other animals, the wants and desires of his body, and consulting his present gratification and immediate interest. But it is not designed that he shall continue thus.

He is made for something better and higher He has a nobler nature and nobler interests. He must learn to live for these; and this learning to feel and value his spiritual nature, and to live for eternity; this change from the animal and earthly existence of infancy, to a rational, moral, spiritual existence,—this it is to be born into the spiritual life. This is a renovation of principle and purpose through which every one must pass. Every one must thus turn from his natural devotion to things earthly to a devotion to things heavenly. This change it is the object of the gospel to effect; and we seek no less than this, when we seek the influence of the gospel on our souls.

Now, the persons of whom I am speaking have not yet acquired this new taste and principle. It has made with them no part of the process of education. It is yet to be acquired. They are desirous of acquiring it. Let them first be persuaded of its absolute *necessity*. Until this is felt, nothing can be effectually done. Without it, there will be no such strenuous effort for religious attainment as is necessary to success. Many persons have at times, some have frequently, a certain conviction upon their minds, that they are not passing their lives as they ought, and they make half a resolution to do differently. They are ill content with their condition; they long to be free from the reproaches of conscience; they wish to be assured that their souls are safe. But, although uneasy and dissatisfied, they take no steps towards improving their condition, because they have no proper persuasion of its absolute necessity. They must be deeply convinced of this. They must strongly feel that a state of indifference is a state of danger; that they are on the brink of ruin, so long as they are alienated from God, and governed by passion, appetite, and inclination, rather than a sense of duty. And such is the power of habit, that they in vain hope to be delivered from its bondage, and to become consistent followers of Christ, unless a strong feeling shall lead them to make a resolute, energetic effort. If they allow themselves to fancy that it will be time enough by and by; that, after all, the case is not very desperate, but can be remedied at any time; and that it would be a pity yet to abandon their pleasant vices;—then there is no hope for them. They are cherishing the most dangerous of all states of mind ; a state, which prevents all real desire for improvement, is continually weakening their power of change, and absolutely destroys the prospect of amendment. They must begin the remedy by a persuasion of its necessity. They must feel it so strongly, that they cannot rest content without immediately subjecting themselves to the dominion of religion,—as a starving man feels the necessity of immediately applying to the search for food. No man will give himself to the thoughts, studies, devotions, and charities, of a religious life, who does not find them essential to the satisfaction and peace of his mind, that is, who is satisfied without them. Cherish therefore the conviction of this necessity. Cultivate by every possible means a deep persuasion of the truth, that the service and love of God are the only sufficient sources of happiness; and that only pain and shame can await him who withholds his soul from the light and purity for which it was made.

Feeling thus the importance of a religious life, let them next be persuaded that its attainment is entirely in their power. It is but to use the faculties which God has given them, in the work and with the aid which God has appointed. No one will venture to say that he is incapable of this. A religious life, as we have seen, grows out of the relations in which man stands to God and his fellow men; and as he is made accountable for the performance of the duties of these relations, it is impossible that he is not created capable of performing them. It were as reasonable to urge that a child cannot love and obey its father and mother, as that a man cannot love and obey God.

Yet it so happens, that some profess to be deterred from a religious course, by the apprehension that it is not in their power; it is something which it must be given them to do; a work which must be wrought in them by a supernatural energy; they must wait till their time has come. But every apology for irreligion, founded on reasons like this, is evidently deceptive. It proceeds upon wrong notions respecting the divine aid imparted to man. That this aid is needed and is given in the Christian life, is a true and comforting doctrine. But that it is to supersede human exertion, that it is a reason for indolence and religious neglect, is a false and pernicious notion,—countenanced, I will venture to affirm, by no one whose opinion or example is honored or followed in the Christian church. On the contrary, all agree in declaring with the Apostle, that while 'God works in us to will and to do,' we are to 'work out our own salvation;' and to do it with 'fear and trembling,' because, after all, these divine influences will be vain without our own diligence.

In some persons, this notion takes the form of a real or fancied humility. They fear lest they be found seeking salvation through their own works, and relying on their own merits. But what a strange humility this, which leads to a disregard of the divine will, and disobedience to the divine commands; which virtually says, 'I will continue in sin that grace may abound!' Let me ask, too, Who will trust to receive salvation without actual obedience? Where is it promised to those who will do nothing in the way of self-government and active virtue? Where is it offered to any, but those who seek it by 'bringing forth fruits meet for repentance,' and by 'patient continuance in well-doing?'

And let none fear lest this make void the grace of God. For how is it that grace leads to salvation? Is it by arbitrarily fitting the soul for it, and ushering it into heaven without its own coöperation? Or is it not rather by opening a free highway to the kingdom of life, through which all may walk and be saved? This is what the Saviour has done; he has made the path of life accessible and plain, has thrown open the gate of heaven, has taught men how to enter in and reach their bliss. Whoever pursues this path, and enters 'through the gate into the city,' is saved by grace. For though he has used his own powers to travel on this highway, yet he did not establish that highway; nor could he have traversed it without guidance and aid; nor could he have opened for himself the door of entrance. Heaven is still a free gift, inasmuch as it is granted by infinite benignity to those who did not, do not, and cannot deserve it. Yet there are certain conditions to be performed. And to refuse the performance of those conditions, on the plea that you thus derogate from the mercy of God, and do something to purchase or merit happiness, is a madness which ought to be strenuously opposed, or it will leave you to perish in your sins.

These two things, then, may be regarded as axioms of the religious life; first, that a man's own labors are essential to his salvation; second, that his utmost virtue does nothing toward purchasing or meriting salvation. When he has done all his duty, he is still, as the Saviour declares, but an 'unprofitable servant.' He has been more than recompensed by the blessings of this present life. That the happiness of an eternal state may be attained, in addition to these, is a provision of pure grace; and it is mere insanity to neglect the duties of religion through any fear lest you should seem to be seeking heaven on the ground of your own desert. Virtue would be your duty, though you were to perish forever at the grave; and that God has opened to his children the prospect of a future inheritance infinitely disproportioned to their merit, is only a further reason for making virtue your first and chief pursuit.

It is true there is great infirmity in human

nature, and you will find yourself perplexed and harassed by temptations from without and within. Passion, appetite, pleasure, and care, solicit and urge you, and render it not easy to keep yourself unspotted from the world. But what then? Does this excuse the want of exertion? Is this a good reason for sitting idly with folded arms, and saying, It is all vain; I am wretchedly weak; I cannot undertake this work, till God gives me strength? Believe me, there is no humility in this. Think of yourself and of your deserts as humbly as you please; but to think so meanly of the powers God has given you, as to deem them insufficient for the work he has assigned you, is less humility than ingratitude and want of faith. Nothing is truer than this,—that your work is proportioned to your powers, and your trials to your strength. 'No temptation hath taken you but such as is common to man; but God is faithful, who will not suffer you to be tempted above that ye are able; but will, with the temptation, also make a way to escape, that ye may be able to bear it.' Here is the manifestation of peculiar grace; when a sincere and humble spirit, in its earnest search for the true way, encounters obstacles, hardships, and opposition, at this moment it is, that aid from on high is interposed. The promise to Paul is fulfilled, 'My strength is made perfect in weakness.' 'The spirit helpeth our infirmities.' Let it be, then, that human nature is weak; no work is appointed greater than its power, and it 'can do all things through Christ who strengtheneth.'

Be thoroughly persuaded, therefore, that the work before you is wholly within your power. Nothing has a more palsying effect on one's exertions in any enterprise, than the doubt whether he be equal to it. Something like confidence is necessary to enable him to pursue it vigorously and perseveringly. It is as necessary in action, as the Apostle represents it to be in prayer. 'He that wavereth or doubteth is like a wave of the sea, driven by the wind and tossed.' But when he has confidence, as the Christian may have, that his strength is equal to his task, that he cannot fail if he resolutely go forward, and that all hinderances must disappear before a steady and industrious zeal, which leans upon God, and is strong in the power of the Lord,—then he presses on with alacrity, encounters trials without alarm, and is 'steadfast, immovable, always abounding in the work of the Lord; knowing that his labor is not in vain in the Lord;' for that nothing but his own fault can bar him out of heaven, or cause him to fail of eternal life.

And all this is perfectly consistent with the deepest humility, and the profoundest sense of dependence on God.

CHAPTER III.

THE STATE OF MIND IN WHICH THE INQUIRER SHOULD SUSTAIN HIMSELF.

All this, I say, is perfectly consistent with the deepest humility and most unassuming dependence upon God. If it were not, it would be false and wrong; for a humble and dependent disposition is a prime requisite in the Christian; a grace to be especially cultivated at the beginning of the religious course. It is concerning this state of mind that we are now to speak.

Deep religious impressions are always accompanied by a sense of personal unworthiness, and not unfrequently commence with it. It is man's acquaintance with himself, which leads him most earnestly to seek the acquaintance of God, and to perceive the need of his favor. The sense of sin, the feeling that his life has not been right, that his heart is not pure, that his thoughts, dispositions, appetites, passions, have not been duly regulated, that he has lived according to his own will, and not that of God, that, if taken from his worldly possessions, he has no other object of desire and affection to which his heart could cling, if called to judgment for the use of his powers and privileges, he must be speechless and hopeless; all this rises solemnly to his mind, and sinks him low under a sense of ill desert and shame. He sees that he might have been, ought to have been, better; that he might have been, ought to have been, obedient to God, and a follower of all that is good. He cannot excuse himself to himself. Every effort to palliate his guilt, only shows him its aggravation; and he cries out, with the penitent prodigal, 'Father, I have sinned against heaven, and in thy sight, and am no more worthy to be called thy son.' He has offended against knowledge and opportunity, and in spite of instruction and warning. He looks back to the early and innocent days, when, if his Saviour had been on earth, he might have taken him to his arms, and said, 'Of such is the kingdom of God.' But, alas! how has he been changed! He has parted with that innocence, he has strayed from the kingdom of heaven, he has defiled and lost the image of his Maker. While he dwells on this thought of what he was, and what he might have become, and contrasts it with what he is, he is filled with remorse. He exaggerates to himself all his failings, paints, in blacker colors than even the truth, all his iniquities, counts himself the chief of sinners, and is almost ready to despair of mercy.

When the mind is strongly agitated in this way, it is surprising how the characters of very different men become, as it were, equalized. Of many individuals, differing in the most various ways as regards the number and nature, the magnitude and circumstances of their offences, and most widely separated in the actual scale of demerit, each, at such a season, regards himself as the most guilty of men. Sometimes the high-wrought expressions, in which the victim of remorse vents the excruciating anguish of his mind, are accounted affectation and hypocrisy. But there can be no good reason to doubt that they are entirely sincere. The man honestly describes himself as he seems to himself at the time. He *is*, in his own eyes, the wretch he draws. And this is very easily explained. He sees at one view all his past sins, open and secret, his thoughtlessness, ingratitude, negligence, and omissions, his depraved inclinations, evil desires, and cherished lusts, which no one else knows, and which no one else could compare, as he can, with his privileges and obligations. All these he sets by the side, not of the hidden and private life of others, but of their decent public demeanor. He compares them, too, not with the standard of worldly, outward morality, but with the strict, searching, holy requisitions of the law of God. And in such a comparison, at such a moment, he cannot but regard himself as most unworthy and depraved.

And we need not be too anxious at once to correct this feeling. The abasement is well; for no one can feel guilt too strongly, or abhor sin too deeply. The time will come, when he will learn to follow the direction of the Apostle, and 'think of himself soberly, as he ought to think.' But at this first fair inspection of the deformities of his character, it is not to be expected that he should make his estimate with perfect sobriety. Only let every thing be done to guide, and soothe, and encourage him, and nothing to exasperate

4

his self-condemnation, or drive him to insanity or despair.

But such a state of mind as I have described, though not uncommon, and by many cherished as the most desirable and suitable at the commencement of the religious life is by no means universal at that period, and cannot be regarded as essential. The experience of different individuals in this respect greatly varies, and is much affected by temper and disposition, as well as by other circumstances. Many excellent Christians have never been subjected to those violent and torturing emotions, which have shaken ana convulsed others. Their course has been placid and serene, though solemn and humble. They have felt their sin, and have mourned beneath it, and in deep humiliation have sought its forgiveness; but without any thing of terrified emotion or gloomy despondency. They have been gently won to truth by the mild invitations of parental love, without needing the fearful denunciations of punishment and wrath to awaken them. This difference among individuals is owing partly, as I said, to constitutional difference of temperament, which renders it impossible that the same representations should affect all alike; and partly to the different modes in which religion is presented to different minds; having first appeared to some in its harsher features, as to the Jews on Sinai, and to others in the milder form of a Saviour's compassion But however this may be, and however the humiliation of one may wear a different complexion from that of another, it is a state of mind sincere and heartfelt in all, to be studiously cherished, and to be made permanent in the character.

In the beginning of the Christian life, this feeling assumes the form of anxiety, as it afterward leads to watchfulness. This word may, perhaps as well as any, describe the state of those for whom I am writing. They are *anxious* about themselves, about their characters, their condition, their prospects. They are anxious to know what they shall do to be saved, and to gain satisfactory assurance that they shall be pardoned and accepted of God. This is a most reasonable solicitude. What can be more reasonable than such a solicitude for the greatest and most lasting good of man? What more becoming a rational creature, whose eternal welfare is dependent on his own choice between good and evil, than this desire to know and pursue the right? this earnest thoughtfulness respecting his condition? and this inquiry for the true end of his being? If a person, hitherto thoughtless, is in this state of mind, he is to be congratulated upon it. We are to be thankful to God in his behalf, that another immortal soul is awake to its responsibility, and seeking real happiness. We would urge him to cherish the feelings which possess him; not with melancholy despondency; not with superstitious gloom; not with unmanly and unmeaning debasement; but with thoughtful, self-distrusting concern, with deliberate study for the path of duty, and a resolute purpose not to swerve from it.

Remember that much depends, I might say, every thing depends, on the use you make of this your present disposition. Be faithful to it, obey its promptings, let it form in you the habit of devout reflection and religious action, and all must be well. The issue will be the Christian character, and the soul's salvation. But refuse to cherish this disposition, drive it from you, smother and silence it, and you will probably do yourself an everlasting injury. It is like putting out a fire which has just been lighted, and which may with difficulty be kindled again. It is trifling with the sensibility of conscience, it is bringing hardness upon your heart; and there is less prospect that you will afterward arrive at an habitual and controlling regard for your religious interests. This it is to 'quench the spirit.'

Be sensible, therefore, that this is a critical moment in the history of your character, that it is in many respects the decisive point at which your destiny is to be determined. For now it is, in all probability, that the bias of your mind is to be determined for good or evil. Be sensible, then, how necessary it is that you keep alive, and cultivate by all possible means, this tenderness of heart. Avoid every pursuit, engagement, and company, which you find to be inconsistent with it, or unfavorable to it, or tending to destroy it. Scenes at other times innocent, should now be shunned, if they operate to turn the current of your affections; for you are engaging in a great work, *the giving your heart a permanent bias toward God*, and it ought not to be interrupted. While this is doing, you can well afford to withdraw from many scenes you might otherwise frequent, and indeed you can ill afford the risk of exposing yourself to their influence.

It may be well to observe another caution. Say nothing of your thoughts and feelings to any, but one or two confidential friends. Many a religious character has been spoiled in the forming, by too much talk with too many persons. The best religious character is formed in retirement, by much silent reflection, and private reading and prayer. What the soul needs above all things, is to commune with itself and with God; then it is established, strengthened, settled. But if a man go out from his closet, and seek for instruction and guidance by talking with all who will talk with him, he fritters away his feelings; his frame becomes less deeply and essentially spiritual; words take the place of sentiment; and he is very likely to become a talkative, fluent, superficial religionist, with much show of sound doctrine, and a goodly readiness of sound speech, but without substantial principle. Shun, therefore, rather than seek, much communication with many persons. But some counsel and encouragement you may need. Apply, therefore, to your minister. He is your legitimate and true counsellor, and he will be glad, in friendly and confidential intercourse, to lead you on. You may have also some pious friend, to whom, possibly, you may unbosom yourself more freely than you have courage to do to your minister; and he may, in some particulars, give you aid, which the situation of the pastor may put it out of his power to afford. In this manner, feel your way along quietly, silently, steadily. Let the growth within you be like that of the grain of wheat, which germinates in secret, and springs up without observation, and attracts little notice of men, till it shows 'the ear and the full corn in the ear.' Be anxious to establish yourself firmly in the power of godliness, before you exhibit its form.

In connexion with this, it may be well to add a caution on a kindred point. Do not spend too much time in public meetings. You will, of course, be desirous to hear the preaching of the gospel. You feel as if you could not hear it too often or too much. You wonder that preaching should never before have seemed so interesting. You listen with unstopped ears; and prayers, hymns, and sermons, fall upon your spirit as if you had been gifted with a new sense. It is well that it is so. By all means cherish this ardent interest in public worship. But do not indulge it to excess. Let your moderation be seen in giving to this its proper place and importance in your time and regard. It is not the only religious enjoyment or means of improvement in your power; and it may possibly be mere self-indulgence which carries one from meeting to meeting. Remember that no duty towards others is to be neglected in the search for personal improvement; this would be sin. And it is at times a higher duty to attend to your family, to be with your friends, to instruct your children, to consult the feelings and yield to the prejudices of a husband or wife, a parent, brother or sister, than it is to pursue your own single advantage, it may be your own gratification, by going out to social worship. And if it be your object to please God or discipline your own spirit, you will better effect that object by this exercise of self-denial, than by doing what would give uneasiness to others, and perhaps even alienate them from you, and render them hostile to religion itself. The advice of the Apostle to wives is in force on this point, and is equally applicable to the other social relations: 'Ye wives, be in subjection to your own husbands; that if any obey not the word, they may, without the word, be won by the conversation of the wives; while they behold your chaste conversation coupled with fear.'

Be warned, therefore, against this error. And what are you to lose by the course which I recommend? Believe me, however much may be gained by the sympathy and excitement of a public assembly, quite as much is gained by the sacrifice of your inclinations to duty and to the feelings of others, and by the silent, unwitnessed exercises of retirement, which no one can forbid you. Look not at the present moment, but at the end. Your desire is to form a genuine, solid, thorough, permanent character of devotion. Well; try to form it wholly in the excitement, and beneath the external influence, of public meetings, and it will be such a character as can exist only in such scenes. Your piety will always need the presence and voice of men to keep it alive, and, unsustained by them, will sink away and die. This, at least, is the danger to be apprehended; and experience declares that it is no slight one. But form your character in private, build it up by the action of your own mind, under the direction of the Bible, and by intercourse with the Father of spirits,—and then it will always be independent of other men and of outward circumstances. It will be self-sustained on a foundation which man and earth cannot shake, alike powerful in the solitude and in the crowd, and immovable in steadfastness, though all other men prove false, and faith have fled all other bosoms. It is such a piety that belongs to the Christian; it is such that you are to seek; and you may well be apprehensive of failure, if you neglect this salutary caution.

CHAPTER IV.

THE MEANS OF RELIGIOUS IMPROVEMENT.

The means to be used in order to render permanent your religious impressions, and promote the growth of your character, are now to be considered. They may be arranged under the following heads:—Reading, Meditation, Prayer, Hearing the word preached, and the Lord's Supper.

I. Reading.

I begin with the more private means; and I speak of reading first, because it is in the perusal of the Scriptures that the beginning of religious knowledge is to be found. It is they which testify of Christ, and have the words of eternal life. It is they which make wise unto salvation. And it is through a devout acquaintance with them, that the mind and heart grow in the knowledge and love of God, and that the dispositions are formed which prepare for heaven. Every one may read the

Bible, and, such is its plainness and simplicity in all matters pertaining to life and godliness, that if he be able to read nothing else, he may yet learn all that is essential to duty and acceptance. Hence it has happened, that many, to whom circumstances have interdicted all general acquaintance with books, have gathered, from their solitary study of the Bible alone, a wisdom which has expanded and elevated their minds, and a peace which has raised them above the darkness and trials of an unhappy worldly lot.

There are those whose condition in life is such, that they have very little time or means to devote to books, and it were vain to recommend to them that they should seek instruction beyond the sacred pages, and the simplest elementary works of devotion. While, therefore, it is the undoubted duty of every one to make the utmost possible progress in religious knowledge, no one is to be condemned for that omission of study and ignorance of books which are rendered unavoidable by circumstances. We must make a distinction, it has been truly said, between that which is the duty of all, and may be done by all, that is, a careful and devout perusal of the Scriptures, and that which is the duty, because within the ability, only of a more limited number,—the study of other sources of knowledge and virtue. These every one must pursue in proportion to his leisure and means.

The class of those who have the leisure and means is large and numerous; it is to be wished that they were more alive to their obligation to improve themselves accordingly. I know not how it happens, that serious and devout persons are so content to be ignorant on those great topics which they truly feel to transcend all others in importance. It certainly deserves their consideration, whether this indifference be either creditable or right. Capacity and opportunity form the measure of duty; and if they have received the power and means of cultivating their minds and adding to their treasures of truth and thought, they should regard it as an intimation that this is required of them. They should not esteem it enough to be sincere and conscientious; they should desire to be well-informed; well-informed respecting the interpretation of the more difficult and curious portions of holy writ.

respecting the history and transmission of the records of their faith, the fortunes of the church in successive ages, the effects of their religion and of other religions on the world, the past and present state of religious opinions, the past and present operations of Christian benevolence, the means of doing good, and the lives, labors, and speculations of the eminent professors of their faith. Now, all this is to be known only through books; and in order to attain it, a judicious selection of books, and an appropriation of certain seasons for reading, are primarily requisite. The bare importance and interest of these subjects ought to be a sufficient inducement to the adoption of this course.

There are many other considerations which render it worthy of attention. The preaching of divine truth becomes far more profitable to those who have prepared themselves for it by the information thus acquired. Words are used in the pulpit, modes of speech occur, allusions are made, and facts and reasonings referred to, which presuppose an acquaintance with certain subjects, and which are entirely lost to those who never read. The better a hearer is furnished with preliminary knowledge, the greater pleasure will he derive from the pulpit; because the better will he understand and appreciate the sentiments expressed. At present, such is the uninformed character of a large portion of ordinary congregations, that a minister is compelled to pass by many modes of illustration, and many representations of truth and duty, because they would be to a great majority unintelligible, and therefore unprofitable. Instead of going on to perfection in the proclamation of higher and wider views, he is compelled, as the Apostle complained in a similar case, to confine himself 'to the first principles of the oracles of God.' Some teachers, unwilling or unable thus to adapt themselves to the actual stature of their hearers' minds, pursue their own modes of thought and expression, without regard to their audience; and, while they gratify a few reading and thinking men, leave the mass of the people uninstructed and unaffected. Herein is a sad error. But if the preacher must adapt himself to the hearers, the hearers ought to prepare themselves for the preaching. This is to be done by greater familiarity with religious books. They would then be ready for higher and more extensive themes, and for a wider scope of illustration, while the preacher would cease to feel himself fettered. At present, warmed and filled, as his mind must often be, by large contemplation and exalted study, he sometimes unconsciously speaks that which is an unknown tongue to the unlettered man, though delightful and wholesome to him whose habits of reading have prepared him to receive it.

Further still. It might do for mere men of the world, who professedly seek only worldly good, and hold of little worth the goods of the mind,—it might do for *them* to neglect books and thinking, and spend all their precious leisure in idle recreations. They are living for the body. But it is the distinction of the Christian, that he lives for the soul, for his intellectual and moral nature, for that part of him which is noblest now, and which alone shall live for ever. He has passed out of the animal, into the spiritual, life. It is not for him to omit or neglect any suitable means of intellectual or moral cultivation. He is guilty of criminal inconsistency, he is a traitor to his own mind, if he refuse to nourish it, systematically, with knowledge and truth. To keep it inactive and ignorant, is to keep it degraded. Jesus lived and died for it, that it might attain the truth, and that the truth might make it *free*. But what is the freedom of the mind bound in the fetters of ignorance? Freedom and elevation can come to it only through knowledge, and one chief fountain of knowledge is books. These inform and excite it, and furnish food for thought. Thought is exercise; it is to the mind what motion is to the body. Without it, there is neither health nor strength. And when God has graciously ordered that your lot should be cast amid the abundance of books, where you need only put forth your hand and be supplied; when he thus makes easy to you that intellectual and moral attainment which is the soul's dignity and happiness; I see not how you can answer it to your conscience, if you do not sacredly devote to this object a certain portion of your leisure.

In regard to the quantity of time to be thus employed, no uniform rule can be given. Men vary so much in occupation, opportunity, and leisure, that, while one may easily command hours, another can with difficulty secure minutes. On this point every one must be left to the decision of his own conscience Inquire of that, impartially and seriously, and then determine how large a portion of time you can daily give to this great object. I believe it may be laid down as certain, that most persons may afford to it a great deal more than they imagine. Some make no effort to do any thing, because they can effect so little that they account it not worth the effort. But they should remember, that duty does not consist in doing great things, but in doing what we can; and that, if they would redeem from the hurry of business and the relaxation of sleep one quarter of an hour a day, it would be a more praiseworthy offering than the many hours which are given by others. Even five minutes a day would be worth something, would be invaluable to one who was earnestly bent on using it. It would amount in a year to about thirty hours; and who will say that it is not better to improve the mind for thirty hours than not at all? But I am persuaded that there is scarcely any one, however engrossed in necessary cares, who may not find much more time than this—who may not find an hour a day. By greater care of the minutes which he wastes, by abridging a little from his meals, a little from his pleasures, and a little from his sleep, it would be easily accomplished. If one be in earnest, as he should be, if he seek for wisdom as for gold, and for understanding as for hid treasure, it will be no impossible thing to find the requisite time. Few men but could readily gain an hour a day, if they were to gain by it a dollar a day. Indeed, it is often seen, in actual life, that a person, to whom religion has become an object of deep concern, contrives to devote to his books more time than this, though before he would have thought it impossible. Nothing is wanting but the 'willing mind.' If one feel the necessity, every thing else will give way. Rather than remain ignorant and without progress in the truth, he will cheerfully watch an hour later at night, and rise an hour earlier in the morning. The gain to the mind will more than balance the inconvenience to the body.

You may regard it, then, as some proof of

the sincerity and earnestness of your desire for improvement, if you find yourself able to appropriate a certain portion of time to profitable reading. It is important that you select for this purpose those hours which shall be least liable to interruption, and that you allow nothing to infringe upon them. Keep this as holy time. Be punctual and faithful to it, as the banker to his hours of business.

There are seasons in every one's vocation, at which his business is less pressing than at others; and there are also seasons of leisure, which he feels at liberty to take for recreation and amusement. As you will have lost all taste for frivolous amusement and unprofitable pleasures, you will be able to devote all such seasons to the improvement of your mind; and, instead of the theatre and the ball-room, from which you would have returned fatigued in body and distracted in mind, and to some extent unfitted for duty, you will enjoy the converse of the great minds which have blessed the world, and, after filling your soul with their thoughts, will go back to your ordinary duty with a spirit refreshed and invigorated, and a body unwearied. During the season of long evenings, especially, when so many are hurrying from diversion to diversion, as if this long leisure were provided them only that they may contrive how ingeniously they can throw it away,—you will perceive that you have a most favorable opportunity for pursuing extensive researches, and making large acquisitions of knowledge. Evening after evening, in your own quiet retirement, you will sit down to this instructive application. By this diligence what progress may you make! what volumes may you master! to what extent may you penetrate the secrets of science, acquire a knowledge of history and of letters, and become enriched with those great and various treasures of intellect, which are subservient to the growth of the mind and the glory of God! You will thus be using time for the purpose for which it was given,—the ripening and perfecting of your immortal mind; and, at all intervals of release from duty to others, will make it your happiness to be thus performing a great duty to yourself.

In your selection of books, the Bible will, of course, hold the first place. This is to be read daily, and to be your favorite book. Remember, however, that it may be perused in such a manner, that it were better never to have opened it. If studied inattentively, for form's sake, or only for the purpose of gathering arguments to support your opinions, it is read irreligiously, and therefore unprofitably. You must habitually regard it as uttering instructions with a voice of authority, of which you are earnestly to seek the true meaning, and then submissively to obey them. You must never forget that your hopes of right instruction are suspended on the simplicity and fidelity with which you receive those holy words; and as they were written expressly to make you wise unto salvation, no inferior purpose must distract your attention from this.

You will therefore always have in view two objects—to understand the book, and to apply it to your own heart and character.

The study of the Bible, for the purpose of understanding it, is an arduous labor. Dr. Johnson said of the New Testament, "It is the most difficult book in the world, for which the labor of a life is required." No book requires greater and more various aid. Its thorough interpretation is a science by itself;

and you must ask of those, in whose judgment you confide, to point out the requisite helps for this interesting investigation; to enable you to reach the pure text, and arrive at the meaning of every passage as it lay in the mind of the writer. Recollect that a passage standing by itself may bear a very good meaning, which yet was not the meaning designed; and make it a sacred rule, not to receive or quote it in any other sense than that which belongs to it in its original place. The neglect of this rule has occasioned much misinterpretation and misapplication of scripture; and some passages have come to be familiarly understood and cited in senses altogether foreign from their proper import. This is a perversion; and it is an immense evil to have wrong ideas thus fastened upon the language of the sacred writers.

And be not afraid of examining the text scrupulously, and employing the utmost energy of your mind in discovering and determining its true sense. It is a duty to do this. You can decide between opposing and possible interpretations only by applying your own mind to judge between them; and the more keenly, impartially, and fearlessly you proceed, the greater the probability that your decision will be correct. On this point some persons greatly err. They seize on the first meaning which presents itself to their minds, or has been presented by another, and resolutely abide by it; they refuse to investigate further, lest they should be guilty of irreverently trying the divine word by their own fallible reason. Indulge no such weakness as this. Never, indeed, be guilty for a moment of the insane folly and sin of disputing the authority of revelation, or setting up your reason as a superior light and safer guide. But in deciding upon the meaning of scripture, you cannot use your intellectual powers too much or too acutely. Use them constantly, coolly, impartially, with the best aid you can obtain from human authors, and then you may rest satisfied that you have done your duty,—have done all which you could do toward learning the truth; and if you have accompanied it with prayer for a blessing from the Source of truth and wisdom, you cannot have failed, in any essential point, to ascertain the will of God.

But there is another object,—the application of scripture to the forming of the heart and character. This is a higher object than the other, and may be effected in cases where very little of rigid scrutiny can be made into the dark places of the divine word. Blessed be God, it is not necessary, in order to salvation, that one should comprehend all the things hard to be understood, or be able to follow out the train of reasoning in every Epistle, and restore the text in every corruption. Do all this as much as you can. But when you read, as it were for your life; when you take the Bible to your closet, to be the help and the solitary witness of your prayers; when you take it up as a lamp which you are to hold to your heart, for the purpose of searching into its true state, that you may purify and perfect it;—then put from your mind all thoughts of differing interpretations and various readings, and the perplexities of criticism and translation. You have only to do with what is spiritual and practical. You are no more a scholar, seeking for intellectual guidance, but a sinful and accountable creature, asking for help in duty, and deliverance from an evil world and an evil heart. Read, therefore, as if on your knees. Make your heart feel and respond to every sentiment. Apply to yourself with rigor every precept and warning; and according to the character of the passage, let your mind glow with fervor, and be uplifted in holy adoration and devout gratitude, or be thrilled and humbled by the representations of infinite purity and justice, or melted and borne away by the tones of tender love and long-suffering grace. Suffer yourself to read nothing coldly, when you read for spiritual improvement. You might as lawfully pray coldly. Therefore let your reading be like your prayers,—done with all your heart. And be sensible that it is better to go over one short passage many times, till you fully grasp its sentiment, and grow warm with it, than to run over hastily and unfeelingly many chapters.

You are not to suppose, from what has been said, that you are altogether to separate these two modes of reading the Scriptures. On the contrary, it will greatly aid you in unravelling their true meaning, to carry to their interpretation a devout mind, wakeful to the impression of their moral beauty, and in sympathy with their divine origin; since nothing is truer than this,—that a study is rendered easy by the interest of the affections in it, and that difficulties disappear before the excitement of feeling. And, on the other hand, when you are reading expressly for improvement and devotion, you will recur, without effort, and consequently without interruption, to the results of your cooler inquiry, and spontaneously make use of the interpretations which your critical scrutiny has proved to be just.

The cautions thus briefly sketched are important for two reasons; one, that there is a tendency in him who has become interested in the critical examination of the sacred writings, to continue to read them critically and with a principal regard to their elucidation, when he ought to be imbibing their spirit; and the other, that the perception of this tendency has been an apology to many for not engaging in such inquiries at all. They esteem it better to go on with their crude, unconnected, and undigested knowledge, which in many cases is only ignorance (for where they have not inquired, it is impossible they should know), than to check the fervor of their religious feelings, as they fancy must inevitably be done, by accurate study. But this is a melancholy error. It reminds one of the old pretence that ignórance is the mother of devotion. How can it be rationally supposed, that a careful inquiry concerning the history, the text, and the signification of the Bible, should necessarily alienate the mind from the true spirit of the Bible! I say necessarily, because the tendency alluded to undoubtedly exists; and, however it may be accounted for, it evidently needs to be cautiously guarded against. This may be done. Do it, then, as you value the warmth and fervor of your soul. Do it, always and perseveringly, by daily reading in that frame of spiritual self-application which I have recommended. Thus you will avoid the danger; and while you arrive at enlarged views of the nature, contents, history and purposes of these sacred records, you will retain and increase the susceptibility of your heart to all their representations of duty and heaven.

In regard to the choice of other books, it would take up too much room to enter into all the many considerations which might be started. Let it be sufficient to say in general, that, if you would form a religious character, you are always to have in view the two objects already named,—religious knowledge and moral improvement. Your books, therefore, will belong to one or the other of these two departments; and it would be well to have one of each kind always lying by you in the course of being read. That is, be at all times engaged with two books; one of a moral and devotional character, to keep your frame of mind right, and your feelings in harmony with eternal truth; the other, of an instructive character, to enlarge your knowledge, and extend your ideas concerning God, and man, and truth. Then you will never be at a loss for occupation. You will not fritter away precious hours in 'wondering what you had better do.'

To the better accomplishment of this purpose, it will be well to obtain of your minister, or some competent friend, a list of selected books, in the order in which they should be read. I earnestly recommend this. Many persons read at random, without selection, whatever they may accidentally meet with.

They make no inquiry whether a book be good or bad, worth perusal or not; but, because it lies in their way, or has been read by some friend, they read it. How many miserable volumes of trash are thus devoured! and that, too, by persons who would be alarmed at the suspicion that they are prodigally throwing away their time. But they do not pursue the same random course in other matters. They do not choose their food or clothing of the first thing which accidentally presents itself They take pains, they spend time, they inquire, compare, judge and select only what they deliberately perceive to be best. And when we treat the body thus, shall we have no care for the mind? Shall we leave it to be fed by any food which chance may bring it, and thus expose it to the risk of pernicious nourishment, to the hazard of being made feeble, sickly, and corrupt? I adjure you, fall not into this too common thoughtlessness. Do not take it for granted, that, because it is a printed book, therefore it must be worth reading. Get advice upon the subject, and read systematically; reflecting, that your object is not amusement, but improvement,—improvement of your religious nature; and that you have no more right to run the hazard of poisoning it through a negligent selection of its nutriment, than to destroy your body by similar means. The religious culture of your mind is a most responsible charge; it is to be effected, in no small degree, by the exercise and guidance it shall receive from books; and how will you lift up your head, when the Judge shall inquire concerning your manner of preparing it for his kingdom, if you have provided for its immortal appetite nothing but unarranged and unselected trash, when stores of the choicest kind were profusely spread before you?

It does not fall within my plan to pursue this subject further, or to treat the many questions which may arise on the choice of books, and habits of reading, in general. It may be said in few words, that no work of truth and science, or of elegance and taste, which does not tend to corrupt the morals or create a disrelish for serious thought, need be prohibited to a religious man. Within the limits of this restriction he may freely range. Let him only remember, that even the employment of reading may become mere idleness and wasteful- ness; and that a man may decide respecting his actual principles and character by the character of the books to which he is most attached. He must therefore watch and guard his taste. Then he may find it in his power to cause every hour thus spent to minister to the growth of his best attainments.

II. Meditation.

This is a great and essential means of improvement. It is essential to self-examination and self-knowledge, without which the hope of progress and of virtue is vain. No one can know his own character, or be aware of the dispositions, feelings and motives by which he is actuated, except by means of deep and searching reflection. In the crowd of business and the hurry of the world, we are apt to rush on without weighing, as we should, the considerations which urge us; we are liable to neglect that close inspection of ourselves, and that careful reference of our conduct to the unerring standard of right, which are requisite both to our knowing where we are, and to our keeping in the right way. It is necessary that we sometimes pause and look around us, and consider our ways; that we take observation of the course we are running, and the various influences to which we are subjected, and be sure that we are not driven or drifted from the direction in which we ought to be proceeding. Without this there is no safety.

Meditation, too, is necessary in order to the digesting of religious truth, making familiar what we have learned, and incorporating it with our own minds. We cannot even retain it in our memories, much less can we be fully sensible of its power and worth, except through the habit of reflecting upon it. We cannot have it ready at command, so as to defend it when assailed, or state it when inquired after, or apply it in the emergencies of life, unless it be familiar to us by habitual meditation; so that even reading loses its value if unaccompanied by reflection. The obligations and motives of duty, the promises, hopes and prospects of the Christian, the great interests and permanent realities by which he is to be actuated, are not visibly and tangibly present to him, like the scenes of his passing life; and they must be made spiritually present by deliberate meditation, if he would be guided and swayed by them. Indeed, without this, he must be without consideration or devotion, ignorant of the actual state of his character, and in constant danger of falling a sacrifice to the unfriendly influences of the world.

In attempting, therefore, the acquisition of a religious character, it is important that you maintain an habitual thoughtfulness of mind. It has been said, and with perfect truth, that no man pursues any great interest of any kind, in which important consequences are at stake, without a profound and settled seriousness of mind; and that a man of really frivolous disposition never accomplishes any thing valuable. How especially true must this be, in regard to the great interests of religion and eternity! How can you hope to make progress in that perplexing and difficult work, the establishment of a religious character, the attainment of the great Christian accomplishments, without a fixed and habitual thoughtfulness?—a thoughtfulness which never forgets the vastness and responsibility of the work assigned to man, nor loses the consciousness of a relation to more glorious beings than are found upon the earth. This must be your habit;—something more than an occasional musing and reverie, at set times, when you shall force yourself to the task. It must be the uniform condition of your mind; as much so as solicitude to the merchant, who has great treasures exposed to the uncertainties of the ocean and the foe;—a solicitude, in your case not gloomy, or unsocial, or morose, but thoughtful; so that nothing shall be done inconsiderately, or without adverting to the bearing it may have on your character and final prospects.

Then, besides this general state of mind, there must be, as I have said, allotted periods of express meditation. As the precept respecting devotion is, 'Pray without ceasing,' and yet set times of prayer are necessary: so also, while we say, 'Be always thoughtful,' we must add, that particular seasons are necessary on purpose for meditation. You must set apart certain times for reflection, when you shall deliberately sit down and survey with keen scrutiny yourself, your condition, your past life, and the prospect before you; inquire into the state of your religious knowledge and personal attainments; and strengthen your sense of responsibility and purposes of duty, by dwelling on the attributes and government of God, the ways of his providence, the revelations of his word, the requisitions of his will, the glory of his kingdom, and all the affecting truths and promises which the gospel displays. These are to be subjects of distinct and profound consideration, till your mind becomes imbued with them, and until, filled and inspired by the spiritual contemplation, you are in a manner 'changed into the same image as by the spirit of the Lord.' The proper season for this is the season of your daily devotion; when, having shut out the world, and sought the nearer presence of God, your mind is prepared to work fervently. Then, contemplation, aided by prayer, ascends to heights which it could never reach alone; and sometimes, whether in the body or out of the body it can hardly tell, soars, as it were to the third heaven, and enjoys a revelation to which, at other hours, it is a stranger.

This, however, is an excitement of mind which is rarely to be expected. Those seasons are 'few as angel's visits,' which lift the spirit to any thing like ecstasy. They are glimpses of heaven, which the soul, in its present tabernacle, can seldom catch, only frequently enough to afford a brief foretaste of that bliss to which it shall hereafter arrive. Its ordinary musings are less ethereal; happy, undoubtedly, though oftentimes clouded by feelings of sadness and doubt, and by a sense of unworthiness and sin. But however mixed they may be, they are always salutary. If sad and disheartening, they lead to more vigilant self-examination, that we may discover their cause, and thus rekindle the watchlight that is so essential to right progress. If serene and joyous, they are a present earnest of the peace which is assured to the righteous, and the joy heart which is one of the genuine fruits of ne spirit. Be not, therefore, troubled or cast down (indeed never be cast down, so long as you can say to your soul, Trust in God); be not, I say, disquieted or cast down, because of the inequalities of feeling with which you enter and leave your closet, and the changes from brightness to gloom, from clearness to obscurity, which often pass over your mind. This, alas! is the inheritance of our frail nature. An equal vigor of thought, clearness of apprehension, force of imagination, fervor of devotion, always perceiving, feeling, adoring, with the same vividness and satisfaction, are to be our portion in the world of spirits. Here we see all things, 'as in a glass, darkly'; there we shall see 'face to face.' Here the truths we rejoice in are too often like the images of absent friends, which we strive in vain to bring brightly before the eye of our minds; they are shadowy, indistinct, and fleeting. But there they will be like our friends themselves, always present in their own full form and beauty, to dwell in the mind unfadingly, and constitute its bliss. Be satisfied, then, if you sometimes arrive, in your meditations, at that glow of elevated enjoyment which you desire. What you are rather to seek for, is, a calm and composed state of the affections, an equanimity of spirit, a serenity of temper;—like the quiet which an affectionate child experiences in the circle of its parents and brothers, where it is not excited to ecstasy by the thought of its father's goodness, but lives beneath it in a state of equal and affectionate trust. Like this should be the habitual experience of the Christian; and if it be thus with you, let not occasional dullness or darkness, coming over your spirit in its religious hours, dishearten or distress you.

This I say, because many persons of truly devout habits have unquestionably suffered much from this cause. In the natural fluctuations of the animal spirits, or the nervous system, or the bodily health, they sometimes find themselves cold at heart, and seemingly insensible to religious considerations. It seems to them that their hearts have waxed gross, that their eyes are closed, and their ears become dull of hearing. In vain do they read and think; they cannot arouse themselves to any thing like a 'realizing sense' of these great objects; but regard with a stupid unconcern what at other times has been the source of their chief enjoyment. But let the humble and timid believer be of good cheer. This is not always a sign of guilt, or of desertion by God. It may be traced to the original and unavoidable imperfection of human nature ; it is to be lamented as such, but not to be repented of as sin ; and one may not expect to be relieved from it, till the soul is freed from the body. Let him watch the course of his mind, and he will find the same inequality of feeling to exist upon other subjects. He does not at all times take an equal interest in his ordinary concerns, nor does he at all times feel the highest warmth of affection toward his parent, friend, or child. Let him observe others, and he will discover the same variations in them. They will confess it to be so. The oldest and most established Christians will describe themselves to have passed their whole pilgrimage in this state of fluctuation. Read the private journals of distinguished believers, and you find in them frequent complaints of lukewarmness, indifference, and deadness of heart. They mourn over it, they bewail it, they strive against it, and yet it adheres to them as long as they live. It is not, therefore, your peculiar sin, but a common infirmity. Regard it in this light ; and do not let it destroy your peace of mind, or lead you to overlook the rational evidence that your heart is right with God.

But also, on the other hand,—for the Christian's path is hedged in with dangers on every side, and in trying to escape from one it is easy to rush into another,—take heed that you do not unwarrantably apply this consolation and make this excuse to yourself in cases in which you really deserve blame. Do not let this apology, which is designed only for the comfort of the humble and watchful, be used by you as a cover for negligence and sinful self-confidence. Remember that your unsatisfactory state of religious sensibility may be possibly your fault; and you are not to presume that it is otherwise, until you have faithfully searched and tried. Have you not, for a time, been unreasonably devoted to amusement, or engrossed by unnecessary cares, so as to have neglected the watching of your heart? Have you not for a season been thoughtless, light-minded, frivolous, and careless of that devout reference to God, by which you should always be actuated? Have you not engaged in some questionable undertaking, or allowed yourself in sloth or self-indulgence, or cherished ill feelings toward others, or permitted your temper to be kept irritated by some unimportant vexations, or let your imagination run loose among forbidden desires? Ask yourself such questions; and perhaps in the nature of your recent occupations you may detect the cause of your present listlessness. If so, change the general turn of your life. In the words of Cowper's hymn, it is only 'A closer walk with God,' which can bring back 'the blessedness you once enjoyed.' Now, your heart is desolate and unsatisfied; you find in it 'an aching void, which God alone can fill;' and it is only by renewing your acquaintance with him, that you can renew your peace.

But, after all, remember that you are to judge of the real worth of these seasons, not by your enjoyment of them as they pass, not by the luxury or rapture of your contemplation, but by their effect upon your character and principles, by the religious power you gain from them toward meeting the duties and sufferings, the joys and sorrows, the temptations, trials and conflicts of actual life. Meditation is a means of religion; not to be rested in as a final good, nor allowed to satisfy us, except so far as it imparts to the character a permanent impress of seriousness and duty, and strengthens the principles of faith and self-government. If it add daily vigor to your resolutions, and secure order to your thoughts, serenity to your temper, and uprightness to your life, then it has fulfilled its legitimate purpose. If, on the other hand, it end in the reverie of the hour, then, however fervent and exalted, it is, comparatively speaking, worthless to yourself and unacceptable to God. Its permanent influence on the character is the true test of its value.

It is easy to see, therefore, that there are three purposes which you have in view; the cultivation of a religious spirit, the scrutiny of your life and character, the renewing of your good purposes.

By the first of these, you are to insure the predominance of a spiritual frame of mind, a perpetual, paramount interest in divine truth, and its incorporation with the frame and constitution of your soul; so that you shall be continually enlarging your apprehensions concerning God, his providence and his purposes, and shall at the same time make them part of the very substance of your intellectual constitution, the pervading and actuating motives of all your life.

By this means religion becomes to the Christian what the spirit of his profession is to the soldier,—the one present thought, motive, and impulse, absorbing all others, and urging him to his one great object by its mastery over all other thoughts, principles, and affections. The other two purposes of meditation which I mentioned, may be described as the surveying and burnishing of the warrior's arms, in preparation for the summons to actual combat; or as the act of the mariner in mid ocean, who every day lifts his instruments to the light of heaven, and consults his charts and his books, that he may learn where he is, and what has been his progress, and whether any change must be made in his course in order to his reaching the intended haven. The warrior who should allow his arms to rust for want of a little daily care, and the mariner who should be shipwrecked from neglect of taking seasonable observations, are emblems of the folly of the man who presses on through life, without ever pausing to scrutinize the principles on which he acts, and rectify the errors he has committed.

This self-examination must be universal; embracing alike the conduct of your external life and the habitual tenor of your mind. You must survey the train of your thoughts, the temper you have sustained, your deportment toward others, your conversation, your employment, the use of your time and of your wealth; you must consider by what sort of motives you are prevailingly guided, what is the probable effect of your example, and whether you are doing all the good which might be reasonably expected of you; you must compare yourself with the example of Jesus Christ, and measure your life by the laws of holy living prescribed in his gospel. And in order that these and other topics may all have their place in the survey, it may not be amiss to keep them by you on a written list. Cotton Mather adopted and recommended the practice of assigning to such inquiries each its particular day of the week; so that every day might have its own topic of reflection, and every topic its due share of attention. Others may find this a useful suggestion.

A renewal of your resolutions is to follow this inquiry. Knowing where you are and what you need, you are to arrange your purposes accordingly. It is a sad error of some to fancy that seeing and acknowledging their faults is all which is required of them. They sit down and bewail them, and in weeping and sorrow waste that energy of mind which should have been exerted in amendment. But it is surely far better, with manly readiness, to rise and act without a tear, than to shed torrents of bitter water, and still go on as before. Regret and remorse naturally express themselves in weeping; but repentance shows itself in action. It may begin in sorrow, but it ends in reformation. And you have little reason to be satisfied with your reflections and your penitence, if they do not issue in prompt and resolute action.

III. Prayer.

As there is no duty more frequently enjoined in the New Testament by our Saviour and the Apostles, so there is none which is a more indispensable and efficacious means of religious improvement, than Prayer; for which reasons it demands particular attention.

The practice of devotion is a sign of spiritual life, and a means of preserving it. No one prays heartily without some deep religious sentiment to actuate him. This sentiment may be but occasionally felt; it may be transient in duration; but the exercise of it in acts of devotion tends to render it habitual and permanent, and its frequent exercise causes the mind at length to exist always in a devout posture. He who truly prays, feels, during the act, a sense of God's presence, authority, and love; of his own obligations and unworthiness; of his need of being better. He feels grateful, humble, resigned, anxious for improvement. He who prays often, often has these feelings, and by frequent repetition they become customary and constant. And thus prayer operates as an active, steady, powerful means of Christian progress.

Indeed nothing effectual is to be done without it That it is a chief duty, even natural reason would persuade us. That it is a condition on which divine blessings are bestowed, Christianity assures us. That it is a high gratification and enjoyment, every one knows who has rightly engaged in it. And that it is of all means of moral restraint and spiritual advancement the most effective, no one can doubt, who understands how powerfully it stirs and agitates the strongest and most active principles of man, and how complete is the dominion which those principles have over his character and conduct. All this is clear and sufficient, without adding the assurance of the Saviour, that it is effectual to draw down spiritual aid from heaven. Add this, and the subject is complcte. It is, both naturally and by appointment, a chief duty of man; from the nature of the soul and the intercourse it opens with God, it is the first enjoyment; and through its own intrinsic power and the promise of Jesus, it is the most effectual instrument of moral and spiritual culture.

Perhaps you have been accustomed to the performance of this duty from your childhood You were early taught to repeat your prayers, morning and evening. Pains were taken to make you understand the nature of the duty, and to give you right impressions in performing it. Perhaps you have retained these impressions, and have continued to this time the practice of sincere devotion. On the other hand, you may have lost those impressions, and become neglectful of the duty. Or perhaps you are so unhappy as never to have received instruction on this head. You have passed through childhood without the practice, and without the sentiment which should inspire it; and now, when awakened to a sense of your responsibility, you find yourself a stranger to the mercy-seat. But, however the case may be, the sense of your religious wants now urges you to devotion; and you are anxious to make that acquaintance with God, which alone can secure you peace. How to perform the duty, how to gain the satisfaction, how to reap the advantage, are points upon which you are anxious to obtain direction.

First of all, let me urge upon you the importance of a plan and of customary seasons for your devotions. Have your settled appointments of time and place, and let nothing interfere with them. Many would persuade you that this is too formal; that you should be left more at liberty; that, as you are to pray always, it is quite needless to assign any special season for the duty. And one may conceive of a person having arrived at so high a measure of spiritual attainment, that his thoughts should be a perpetual worship, and retirement to his closet would bring his mind no nearer to God. But such is at best an infrequent case; at any rate it is not yours,—you are a beginner; it never can be yours, except you use the requisite means of arriving at it; and certainly among the surest means is the custom of setting apart stated seasons for devotion. So that the very reason assigned for neglecting, becomes a strong reason for observing them. You must feed the soul as you do the body, furnishing it with suitable nourishment at suitable intervals. You must keep its armor bright and serviceable, as does the soldier in human warfare, who examines and restores it at a certain hour daily. If it were left to be done at any convenient season a thousand trifling engagements might cause the work to be deferred again and again, till irretrievable injury should accrue. You have too many other engagements and enticements daily and hourly occurring, to make it safe for you to leave this to accidental convenience or inclination. In order to secure its performance, you must put it on the list of your daily indispensable engagements; and, as it is part of your routine at certain hours to breakfast and dine, and at certain hours to attend to the concerns of your household and profession, so also must it be, to retire at certain hours for religious worship. The wisdom and experience of all the religious world insist on this; and it would not be necessary to state it so urgently, if it did not seem to be a notion growing into favor with some, that, as the spirit, and not the form, is the essential thing, it is better not to be burdened with methods and rules, but simply to pray always;—which, there is reason to fear, would in practice be found a precept to pray never.

Assign to yourself therefore some convenient hour, when you shall be secure from interruption, and not hurried by the call of other business. If you are much engaged in active affairs, you may perhaps be unable to secure this, unless you rise for the purpose in the morning, and sit up for it at night. This, then, you must do. Deprive yourself of a few moments' sleep, morning and evening. And I may ask here, whether the multitude of persons who excuse their inattention to religious exercises by their want of time, do not thereby expose themselves to a suspicion of insincerity? For if they were truly in earnest, it would be a very little thing to retire to their chambers fifteen minutes earlier, and to rise from their beds fifteen minutes sooner. If they were aware of the magnitude of the gain, the sacrifice would seem insignificant. Nay, they might even perform the duty upon their beds; there would be no want of time then. And some, who, from the misfortune of poverty, have no place to which they can retire, being compelled to live at every moment in the company of others, should learn to feel that the bed is their closet; that, when lying there, they can 'pray to the Father who seeth in secret;' and that they need make no complaint of want of opportunity, so long as they may follow the Psalmist, who said, 'I remember thee on my bed, and meditate on thee in the night-watches.'

Having, then, your stated times, if you would make them in the highest measure profitable, observe the following rules. First of all, when the hour has arrived, seek to excite in your mind a sense of the divine presence, and of the greatness of the act in which you are engaging. Summon up the whole energy of your mind. Put all your powers upon the stretch. Do not allow yourself to utter a word, to use an expression, thoughtlessly, nor without setting before yourself, in a distinct form, its full meaning. Remember the words of Ecclesiasticus: 'When you glorify the Lord, exalt him as much as you can; for even yet will he far exceed: and when you exalt him, put forth all your strength, and be not weary; for you can never go far enough.' Pour your whole soul, the utmost intensity of your feelings, into your words. One sentence uttered thus is better than the cold repetition of an entire liturgy For this reason, let your prayer be preceded by meditation. In this way make an earnest effort after a devout temper. While you thus muse, the fire of your devotion will kindle, and then you may 'speak with your tongue;' then you may breathe out the adoring sentiments of praise and thanksgiving, the holy aspirations after excellence and grace, the humble confessions of your contrite spirit, the glowing emotions of Christian faith. As you proceed, you will probably find yourself increasing in warmth and energy; especially if you give way to the impulse of your feelings, and do not check them by watching them too closely. To do this chills the current of devotion, and changes your prayer from the simple expression of desire and affection, into an exercise of mental philosophy. Wherefore, having warmed your mind, give it free way, and let its religious ardor flow on. But if, as will often be the case, you find your thoughts wander and your feelings cool, then pause, and by silent thought bring back the mind to its duty; and thus intermix meditation with prayer, in such manner that you shall never fall into the mechanical, unmeaning repetition of mere words.

As your object is not to get through with a certain task, but to pray devoutly, you will find it well to vary your method according to circumstances, and not always adhere to the same mode. I have sometimes suspected, that one cause of the little efficacy of public worship may be the invariable method of conducting it; whereby it is rendered formal, monotonous, and deficient in excitement. But however this may be, it is quite certain that a simi.ar unvaried routine would be extremely injudicious in private devotion. In this respect, a very considerable latitude is desirable. As you are not to consult the wants or the convenience of others, but your own duty alone, you may have a single regard to what shall suit the immediate temper and exigencies of your own mind, without being bound by any prescribed rule as to subject, language, or posture.—You will always have by you the Bible to quicken and guide you. But sometimes the first verse you read may lead you to feelings, thoughts, and prayers, which shall so occupy your soul that you will read no more. And it is better to read but one verse, which thus influences your whole spiritual nature, than to read chapters in the unheedful way that is too often practised. At another time, however, the reading of the Scriptures may be your principal occupation, and your less excited mind may not flow beyond a short ejaculation at the close of each verse. Sometimes you may find it well to assist yourself by a printed or written form; always, however, taking care to leave it, when any sentiment or feeling arises within you which is not there expressed. The main advantage of a form in private is, to suggest thoughts, and stimulate the mind; as soon as it has done this, we should lay it down, and go on of ourselves. Then, presently, if we find it necessary, we may again recur to the form, and make the whole exercise, if we please, an alternate use of the form, and of our own language. In all this we must be guided by the occasion.

Similar varieties may be allowed in regard to the subjects of our devotions. There are some great and leading topics of adoration and supplication, which may at no time be forgotten or omitted. But it cannot be necessary in every prayer to go over the whole field of devotional sentiment. It is best that we confine ourselves principally to those which are most immediately interesting at the time, and seek to render our present circumstances, fortunes, failings, and prospects, the nourishment of our devotion. The temptations of our peculiar lot, our recent trials of temper, fortitude, and faith, the dealings of Providence with our family and friends, the exposure, wants, and improvement of those most dear to us,—these, as they are at other moments of the greatest concern to us, should be the objects upon which we should, first of all, seek the blessing of God. This it is to connect every thing with religion; in this way we shall avoid the error, into which some have fallen, of making religion a wholly independent existence, with no reference to the ordinary duties of active life, and no bearing on its common concerns, and of course exercising no influence upon them. Such persons have exhibited the strange spectacle of two contradictory characters in one man, the one apparently devout, the other immoral. But the consistent Christian will never separate his religion from his life, nor his life from his religion. He will seek to incorporate them most intimately with each other. And this he will effect, in no small degree, by making his daily prayers, not the expression of general principles, and indefinite confession, the recitation of articles of faith, or declaration of vague desires after holiness; but the expression of those sentiments which belong to his peculiar condition, and a perpetual reference to his personal character and circumstances. It is for these and concerning these that he will pray; and therefore his prayers will vary as these do.

So much, in a general way, respecting the subjects of private devotion. Next we may say a few words respecting the posture. This need not be invariably the same. Many have laid stress upon it; but it seems to me there is a certain freedom to be allowed in this particular to those who are invited 'to come boldly to the throne of grace.' Provided we secure the right state of the heart, it can matter little what the attitude of the body may be. There are times when the lowest prostration seems best to express and promote the sentiment of lowly adoration and broken-hearted humiliation in which the worshipper supplicates his Father. But again, in a different tone of spirit, he is prompted to stand erect, and lift up his head and hands, as an attitude most corresponding to the elevated sentiments by which he is filled. While sometimes he feels that in walking to and fro, or sitting with his head leaning upon his hands, he can best summon his mind to spiritual worship. Cecil says, that his oratory was a little walk in the corner of his chamber, where he paced backward and forward as he prayed. Others have been able to be devout only on their knees. What I would briefly urge is, that you be not scrupulous on this head. Allow yourself in any mode. Try various modes. Adopt, from time to time, that which best cultivates and encourages the right tone of feeling. At the same time, you will probably find some truth in the remark, that the adoption of a suitable posture aids the adoption of a suitable frame of mind; that the expression of reverence in the attitude conveys a feeling of reverence to the spirit; for which reason it will be generally best to assume the posture most associated with the sentiments of devotion, and depart from it only when the change may be favorable to engagedness and fervor of mind. The soul may be as truly prostrated when you stand, or walk, or ride, or work, or lie in your bed, as when you kneel before the altar.

Neither be too scrupulous concerning the use of your lips. It is oftentimes as well, or better, to pray mentally, without uttering a sound. Yet at the same time there is danger, if this become our practice, that it will end in turning prayer into meditation, and that our hours of devotion will become hours of musing and reverie. This would be injurious; and therefore we should commonly use articulate language. Our thoughts are so much associated with words, and words with their sounds, that it is not easy to think connectedly and profitably without the use of speech. It is well, as I have before said, to muse for a time; but when, after musing, the fire is kindled within us, as the Psalmist expresses it, then we should 'speak with our tongues.' We shall find this an essential aid in rendering our sentiments and train of thought distinct to ourselves; and in so impressing them on our memories, that we shall be able to employ them afterward for our guidance and comfort. Good sentiments, which merely pass through the mind, but are not put into words, are apt to leave no trace behind them; and he who should habitually indulge himself in thinking his prayers, instead of expressing them, would find it extremely difficult to say what he had prayed for, or to turn to any account in common life the employment of his sacred hours.

Meditation is, in its nature, an act very distinct from prayer, and must be very distinct in its effects. Some effects may be common to the two; but much of the peculiar and the happiest influence of devotion on the character must be lost to the man who allows musing to take the place of prayer. It is one thing to contemplate a blessing and desire it; quite another to ask for it. The latter may require a very different temper of mind from the former; and it is plain that the promise of God is given to those who ask, not to those who desire; to those who employ petition, not those who are content with contemplation. Therefore arrange your thoughts in words; and generally give them a distinct utterance in sound; pausing occasionally for reflection, and being certain that you do not employ words only, but that the thoughts which they express are actually in your mind.

In regard to the choice of words, be not too anxious. Take those which express your meaning, without regard to their elegance or eloquence. You will naturally fall into language borrowed from the Scriptures, and that is always good and appropriate. Only take heed that you do not use it mechanically, and without due consideration of its significance. But when you do not use the terms of scripture, take those which express what you mean, and consider nothing further. I would lay the more stress upon this, because some persons actually plead, as an excuse for the neglect of this duty, that they have no command of language, and cannot readily find correct and proper words. This would be a very good reason for not attempting to pray in public; and it were to be wished that some, who are forward to exhibit themselves in this act, would consider it more seriously. It is an injury to religion, when he, who speaks to God in the public assembly, or the circle of social worship, does it in rude, hesitating, confused, inappropriate, or ungrammatical language. But in private, when you are simply to pour out your heart, and have no witness but Heaven, allow yourself to put aside all solicitude on this head. Speak as you feel, and what you feel; only taking care that your feelings are right, and that you know what they are. Alas! you will often find it a task difficult enough to regulate your feelings, govern your thoughts, repress wandering desires, keep out vain images, and bring your soul to a proper attitude of reverence and love, without the added embarrassment of arranging words by the rules of rhetoric and taste. This is an occupation which interferes with the spirituality of the duty you are performing. I beseech you to disregard it altogether.

As respects times and seasons, it may be considered as a salutary rule, that it is better to pray often than long. There are times, undoubtedly, when the mind is glowing and the heart full, that the exercise may be advantageously continued through a long period, and the disciple, like his Master, may spend the whole night in prayer. It would be a pity to check the current when it flows thus

spontaneously, or to lose the luxury of such a season. There may be occasions, too, when duty and improvement shall seem to demand an extraordinary continuance in devotion. I do not therefore recommend that you should limit yourself to a certain stinted number of minutes. But, as a general rule, do not covet long prayers; rather multiply their number than increase their length. This is the rule of Christ; who insists that we pray often and always, but that we do not pray long. A most wise regulation. For the mind is easily wearied by a long exercise, and is likely to return to it slowly and reluctantly; and in the interval, it is liable to go back, like the swinging pendulum, into a directly opposite state. From which cause it may too readily happen that the extended devotions of the morning shall exhaust the attention of the mind, and produce religious listlessness during the day. Whereas, a shorter act of worship, which should excite without exhausting, which should kindle the fire but not burn it out, would leave a glow upon the feelings, that would abide for hours, and prompt to holy

thoughts and spontaneous acts of worship at short intervals throughout the day. In this manner, the great object of keeping up a religious wakefulness and sensibility is with greater certainty obtained, and the whole current of life more surely colored by the infusion of religious sentiment.

Let this, therefore, be your method. Accustom yourself to what is called ejaculatory prayer; that is, to very frequent petitions and thanksgivings, bursting out from your soul at all times and wherever you may be. Walk with God as you would journey with an intimate friend; not satisfied to make formal addresses to him at stated seasons, but turning to him in brief and familiar speech whenever opportunity offers, or occasion or feeling prompts. Remember that ceremonious addresses are appointed, and are chiefly necessary, on social and ceremonious occasions, when a company of men is together, and many minds are to act at once. They can act and be acted upon simultaneously in no other way; and therefore, in civil and state affairs, as well as in religious, this method is in use But when we come to more private, domestic, confidential intercourse, we abandon these formal and complimentary arrangements, and find it most natural and happy to do as occasion prompts, in a free and unrestrained style of conduct and of speech. Just so it should be in our more private and confidential communion with the great Father of our spirits. The more it is unembarrassed by precise forms and ceremonious appendages, and left to the promptings of the feelings and of the moment, the more appropriate is it to our title of 'children,' and the greater is the felicity which it furnishes.

It has, of course, been implied in the preceding remarks, that all is to be done in the spirit of devotion. In what manner this may be effected, it is necessary to state more distinctly; and the rules to be given for this end will sufficiently explain in what that spirit consists.

First, then, the genuine, effectual prayer is the prayer of Faith; not of words, not of form; not an exercise of the understanding, reasoning on the attributes and dispensations of God, and uttering its judgments on duty; but an address to him, accompanied by a confident persuasion that he hears and regards. 'He that cometh to God,' says the Apostle, 'must believe that he is, and that he is a rewarder of them that diligently seek him.' Of this there must be no doubt on the mind. You must realize that you are actually speaking to him, and he listening to you, as truly as when you address yourself to a visible mortal; and you must have as real a conviction that something depends on the act, and as real a desire to receive what you ask for, as when you make a request for some important favor to a human friend. If you doubt, your prayer is weak and inefficacious. 'Ask in faith,' says James, 'nothing wavering; for he that wavereth is like a wave of the sea, driven with the wind and tossed.' His uncertain and fluctuating mind wants stability, and cannot receive a blessing. Therefore it is added, 'Let not that man think that he shall obtain any thing from the Lord.' May we not suppose, that much of the dissatisfaction attendant on our prayers, and much of their unfruitfulness, is owing to the doubtful, hesitating state of mind in which they are offered? And what can be more miserably destructive of all energy and interest in the employment? If you doubt whether you shall be heard, you will pray timidly and coldly, without courage or spirit. If your prayers are thus lifeless, your conduct will be so too, and all spiritual savor will fade away from your life. Do not, then, allow in yourself this doubtfulness of temper. The most extravagant fanaticism, which sees a visible light descending as it prays, and finds an answer in presentiments and dreams, is not more mistaken, and is far more happy. Give yourself up to the assurance, that they who ask shall be heard, and go 'boldly to the throne of grace.' Jesus, by his invitations and doctrine, has given you a right to this confidence; and it is only in the exercise of it, humbly, but firmly, that you may 'cast out the fear which hath torment.'

Next, your prayer must be fervent; that is, your affections must be engaged and interested in it. You must not barely, as a reasoning philosopher, or well instructed pupil, declare what you coolly judge to be right, and assert that man, in his present relations, ought to seek and do what is right, and that

God, as the Father and Governor, should be adored and obeyed (which is the tenor of the devotional exercises one sometimes hears); but you must set yourself actually to do these things. You can only be said to pray when the sentiment you utter springs from your heart; and, rising above all the arguments and persuasions of the wise, you pour out your feelings, as a little child confides its thoughts to a parent's bosom; thinking only of your own dependence and need, and of God's ability and readiness to succor you, and earnestly aspiring after that purity and piety, which you feel to constitute the excellence and bliss of man. When this fervent glow is upon your mind, you pray in the spirit. Seek for it. Be not content without it.

In the next place, do not allow yourself to grow weary. Persevere; however ill satisfied, however discouraged, persevere. Open the New Testament, and you will see how this is insisted upon, again and again, and by various illustrations. 'That men should always pray, and never faint,' was the great moral of more than one of our Lord's parables; and to 'pray without ceasing' was the corresponding direction of his Apostles. Situated as we are in this world, there is danger that, perceiving little immediate fruit from our devotions, we should relax our diligence in them; first doubting their value, then losing our interest in them, and then ceasing to perform them. But we should recollect, that, in this case, as in all the most important and admirable provisions of Divine Wisdom, it is the order of Heaven to give, not to a single exertion, nor to a few acts, nor even to some continuance of effort, but only to a long, unremitted, persevering effort. We read this lesson every where. Look at that glorious operation of God, by which the sun cherishes and matures the fruits of the earth for the sustenance of its creatures. It is not accomplished by one act, nor by several acts, nor yet by sudden, violent exertions of power. He sends out his beams steadily, day by day, month after month; yet the fruit is still green, the harvest immature; and if, weary with the work, he should abandon it, famine might devastate the globe, when but six days' longer perseverance would see it successful. The whole toil of the season might thus be lost, when a trifling addition only was necessary to render it all-effective. In how many other cases is the same truth illustrated! Will you, then, abandon your prayers, because you do not witness the effect from them which you desire? Will you be discouraged, when, by a little longer continuance, you may receive the full blessing at once? Shall the husbandman 'wait patiently,' and will you, looking for an immortal harvest, lose it for want of patience? No. This is the eternal, immutable rule in regard to all great acquisitions. Piety and virtue, character and immortality, depend upon a long succession of actions, neither of them, taken singly, of essential moment, yet all, in the aggregate, essential to effect the great end in view. Apply this consideration to your prayers, and resolutely persevere.

Thus it is the humble prayer of confident faith, fervent and persevering, from which you are to hope benefit and acceptance.

But you may ask, How shall I know that it is accepted, and with what answer should I be satisfied?

To the first part of this question, there is

but one reply. If you are conscious of having prayed aright, you may be assured that your prayer is accepted. You can have no external evidence of the fact; but the Scriptures every where declare, that a right prayer is certainly accepted. This, then, is a reason for self-examination, and for carefully regulating the state of your mind.

You may imagine, however, that you are rather to judge by the answer to your prayers; and that if, after offering earnest petitions for certain blessings, you find them denied, you are to suppose that your devotions are not accepted.

In regard to this, I observe, that the purpose of prayer is twofold—particular and general; the first, to supplicate certain specific blessings which we need or desire; the second, to obtain the divine favor in general; or, which is equivalent to it, to obtain that state of mind and heart which is always an object of complacency with God, and secures his permanent approbation. Now it is evident, that the latter is an object infinitely more important than the former. It is of no consequence whether your receive certain gifts of health, or safety, or prosperous affairs, in comparison with the importance of attaining that frame of soul which God approves, and which will fit you for heaven. If, then, you have plainly gathered from your devotions the advantage of a religious growth, if you are brought by them nearer to God, formed into the likeness of Jesus Christ, and made superior to the things of earth and sense;—then you have gained the highest objects which man may aspire to, and should feel no dissatisfaction or doubt because inferior blessings are denied. Having received the greater, you should be content not to receive the less. And this is a sufficient reply to the second part of the question stated above: viz. With what answer shall I be satisfied? Be satisfied with that answer which is found in the improving state of your own religious affections; in the peace, serenity, confidence, and hope, which belong to a mind habitually conversant with God, and which God bestows only on such.

I do not mean to say, that other and more specific answers may not be sometimes given; for doubtless the devout mind may often have reason to trace particular blessings, and with a practised eye may trace them, to a source which has been opened in reply to the prayer of faith. When you shall perceive it to be so in your own case, happy will you be; and you will not fail to acknowledge it with suitable gratitude. But what I mean to say is, that this is not what you are habitually to expect; you are not to wait for this in order to the satisfaction of your mind. God feeds his children with spiritual food; and it is one part of his discipline of their faith, to deny them temporal blessings in order to the more abundant bestowal of those that are spiritual; to advance the moral man to perfection through the disappointment or mortification of the outward man. Do not, then, be uneasy, because your prayers may at first view seem inefficacious. The service of truth and virtue is not to be rewarded by the wages of this world's goods. Health, strength, riches, prosperity, are not the best, they are not the appropriate, recompense, for self-denial, humility, benevolence, and purity. The true recompense is eternal and imperishable. If you have this, why be dissatisfied that you have not the other? If you have this, how can you fancy that God has not accepted your prayer?

To which it may be added, that, if you prayed aright, you prayed in the spirit of submission; not only acknowledging, but feeling, the wisdom of Heaven to be greater than your own, and desiring to obtain only such gifts as that wisdom should judge it best to bestow. Such gifts, of course, are granted. If, therefore, you were sincere, you should be content. You are not relieved, perhaps, from the trouble against which you prayed; the evil you fear comes, the good you desire is denied, notwithstanding your earnest supplication. But does it follow that your prayer is slighted? Believe it not. What you designed was, to ask blessings; you named the things which you esteemed such; but at the same time you knew that your judgment was fallible. If God has refused the things specified, it is because in his judgment they would not prove blessings, and he has bestowed in their stead an increase of faith, which is a real blessing. Or perhaps I may say, he has proposed to you a discipline of your faith, which will prove a transcendent good, unless, by your blind discontent and misuse of it, you turn it into a curse.

It will follow from these remarks, that we are to dwell in prayer on topics rather of a spiritual than of a temporal nature; that we should ask such things as relate rather to our character than to our condition, rather to our religious than to our worldly prosperity. For, these being the chief objects of desire and happiness (so much so, that our petitions for earthly good oftentimes receive no reply but in the state of our own minds), it must follow that they should be our chief objects of interest and desire in our exalted hours of communication with God. Our religious addresses in those hours are made up of adoration, thanksgiving, confession, petition. Now, two of these, adoration and confession, relate to spiritual objects exclusively. The other two relate to objects of both a spiritual and temporal character, the blessings and wants of both soul and body. But it is plain that the former far exceed the latter in number and in importance, and should therefore occupy the larger share of attention. If, then, you would do what is most consonant to the nature of the exercise, and your own most real wants; if you would receive blessings corresponding to the petitions you express; you will dwell principally on spiritual and immortal good; seeking first of all, in prayer as at all times, 'the kingdom of God and its righteousness.' You will do this, also, if you would copy the pattern which our Lord has given; for of the seven sentences of the prayer which he taught his disciples, only one has relation to man's temporal condition. You will do it, if you would imitate our great Exemplar and Master, whose recorded prayers have exclusive regard to the welfare of his spiritual kingdom and the bestowment of internal blessings.

And it is not to the example alone of the Saviour that you are to have reference in your prayers. You are also to regard him as the Mediator through whom they are to be offered. It belongs to the system of our religion, that the thought of its Founder should be associated in the minds of its disciples with all that they are and do; with their sense of obligation, and their sentiments of piety. They are 'to do every thing in the name of the Lord Jesus;' with a consciousness of their connexion with him, and of their dependence upon the instruction, motives, and strength, which they have received from him. They are 'to walk by faith in the Son of God.' His image is to be blended with their whole life. Especially is this to be the case in the acts of life which are strictly and peculiarly religious. 'Whatsoever ye ask in my name, believing.' 'Giving thanks unto God and the Father by him.' It is only through his instruction, authority, and encouragement, that they know their privilege of filial worship, and are enabled so to offer it that they may look for acceptance. The hope of pardon on the confession of sin is grounded upon what he has done, suffered, and declared; and the confidence with which the penitent seeks forgiveness and life, is owing to his trust in the word of Jesus, and his being able to lean on him as a friend and advocate, when he casts himself a suppliant before God. Understand, then, that the acceptable prayer is that which is made in the name of the great Intercessor: and let your heart be warmed and imboldened in your devotions by the consciousness of your relation to him 'whom the Father heareth always.'

I will add but two further remarks before closing this topic. First, I have all along assumed, that I am addressing a person sincerely engaged in the pursuit of religious attainments. This sincerity of pursuit is a fundamental requisite, without which all exhortations, means, assistance, sacrifices, will be only thrown away. If, therefore, after having made some effort after a spirit of devotion, in pursuance of the course recommended, you find, as men sometimes do, that you derive from it neither improvement nor satisfaction,.I recommend to you to examine whether you are really in earnest; whether you do, actually in your heart, desire religious improvement; whether, in short, there be not in you a lurking preference for your present state of mind, and an attachment to some passion, taste, or pursuit, incompatible with a zealous devotedness to Christian truth, and a suitable attention to the discipline which it demands. Many are, no doubt, prevented from advancement by secret hinderances of this nature, of whose operation they are not at all aware. If, upon inquiry, you cannot discover that it is so with you, then examine strictly the methods you have pursued, and the observances you have practised. You will probably find that they have been in some particulars injudiciously selected, or improperly or insufficiently attended; that you have failed in a resolute, steadfast, systematic adherence to your own rules; that you have habitually allowed yourself in something wrong, or neglected something right. Look after your mistake. When you shall have discovered and corrected it, you may be certain of securing the improvement you desire.

Secondly, take heed that you do not allow yourself to fancy, that an observance of these or similar rules constitutes all your duty under this head. Do not forget, that the devotion which Christianity teaches is nothing less than perpetually thinking, feeling, and acting, as becomes a child of God,—a perpetual worship. This is the end at which you are to aim;—an end, however, which is not to be attained without the use of means; and the directions in the preceding pages are designed simply to point out some of the means. Some persons do not need such directions. For them they are not designed. But there are others to whom they must be welcome and wholesome. Let such use them, but without forgetting that they are means only. Let them guard, from the first and always, against the idea, that the practice of these will secure the great object, without any further exertion or sacrifice; that to be devout men, they have only to observe stated seasons, and perform stated acts. There cannot be a more pernicious error. It is at variance with the whole nature and spirit of Christianity. God is to be served by the entire life; by its actions as well as its thoughts, its duties as well as its desires, its deeds as well as its feelings.

The religious man must have the frame of his mind and the tenor of his conduct at all times religious; in the market and the family no less than in the closet and the church. Indeed, considering how much more of life is spent abroad in action and trial than is passed in the worship and contemplation of retirement, it is plainly of greater consequence to watch and labor in the world than in private. Besides that it is easier to be religiously disposed for an hour a day, when reading the Bible or kneeling at the altar, than it is to be so during the many other hours which are full of the world's temptations, and when all the irregular passions are liable to be excited. Remember, then, to try your prayers by your life; you may know how sincere they are, by their agreement or disagreement with your habitual sentiments and conduct. Regulate your life by your prayers; in vain do you think yourself religious, if you go with holy words and humble confessions to the Divine presence, but at other times live in thoughtlessness and sin. True religion is a single thing. Devout exercises form a part of its exhibition; holy living forms another part. Unless they exist together, it is to no purpose that they exist at all. To separate them is to destroy the religion. To this consideration, then, let your perpetual and vigilant attention be given; and be satisfied with your hours of devotion only when they exercise a sacred and constant influence over the condition of your mind and life, and have made them holy to the Lord.

IV. Preaching.

From the more private means of religious improvement, we pass to the consideration of those which are in their nature public.

Preaching is a divine institution; and its authority and wisdom have been illustriously justified in the success which has attended it in every age of the church. It is to a publication from the lips of living teachers, that the gospel owes its spread through so large a portion of the globe. At its first introduction, at its reformation, and in its present diffusion, it has been the 'company of the preachers' that has arrested attention to its divine truths, and subdued the hearts of men to its holy power. And it always must be the case, however great may be the efficacy of those more personal instruments of which we have spoken, that the pulpit shall be the main engine for the incitement and instruction of the individual mind, and the maintenance of the power of religion in the Christian world.

Multitudes, however, habitually attend the

preaching of the gospel, with little profit, and with no adequate apprehension of its purpose or value. Habit, thoughtlessness, inattention, worldliness, cause its sublime instructions to be unheeded, and render its powerful appeals unimpressive. It may have been so with you, in times past. But if you are now truly awake to the necessity of studying the improvement of your character, and making God's will the rule of your life, you will listen eagerly to the preaching of his truth, and drink it in as a thirsty man water. I say nothing, therefore, to urge the duty of attendance in the house of prayer. You will esteem it one of your privileges, and will feel that, however imperfectly the word may be dispensed, it is yet full of a divine savor, and profitable to any one who seeks his soul's good rather than his mind's entertainment.

In order to the greatest advantage from this duty, it is well, in the first place, to give heed to the manner in which the other hours of the Sabbath are spent. There can be no doubt that one considerable cause of the inefficacy of preaching is to be found in the circumstance that the remainder of the Sabbath is passed in a manner little likely to prepare the mind for its religious services, and suited to obliterate the impressions received from them. The sentiments excited in holy time, instead of being cherished, are checked and smothered by the uncongenial engagements of the rest of the day; and Sunday becomes at length even a day for hardening the heart, through this habitual resistance of the most solemn truths. For, when exposed to their frequent repetition, if it do not yield to them, it must inevitably become callous to them. This evil you are to guard against, by making the whole occupation of the day harmonize with that portion of it which is spent in public worship. And to do this implies no fanatical recluseness or morose sullenness. It implies nothing but the endeavor of a reasonable man, who finds that the cares of the six days tend to distract his feelings from religion, to counteract them on the day set apart for that purpose. It is only saying, with regard to all worldly occupations, what Burke said of politics in the pulpit;—Six days are full of them, and six days are enough; let us give one day to something better.

You will therefore be careful so to spend your morning hours, that you shall enter the sanctuary with a prepared mind,—already touched with a sense of God, and tuned to his praise. Your reading and your thoughts will be directed to this purpose; and instead of cherishing or inviting vain thoughts and a light state of feeling, by lounging over a newspaper, or a novel, or by conversation on the passing events of the day, you will occupy yourself on such subjects as shall hallow the temper of your mind, and exclude the crowd of impertinent desires. Then you will be ready to join feelingly in the public service of your Maker, and listen profitably to the exhortations of the pulpit.

You have doubtless observed in your own case, and heard it remarked by others. that the same discourse, under different circumstances, seems like a very different thing; that what at one time is listened to with pleasure and interest, at another is heard with indifference. To what can this be owing, but to the variation in the hearer's state of mind? The discourse is the same; but it addresses itself to a soul at one time tuned to the occasion and the subject, and at another tuned to something else. So important is adaptation;—as might be illustrated in a thousand ways. Hence you will study to carry a prepared mind to the hearing of the word, that you may not fail of receiving the utmost edification. Otherwise you may sit under the most powerful ministry, and hear divine truth dispensed with an eloquence worthy of angels, and yet sit unmoved. It can be powerful to your heart, it can effectually promote your progress in the Christian life, only through your own preparation to receive it, and in proportion to that preparation.

Let me also caution you to remember, that there is good and important matter belonging to every subject which the pulpit may treat; and it is very unwise (to use the mildest expression) to turn away dissatisfied, because a sermon does not happen to fall in with the state of your feelings. Hearers are often guilty of great injustice in this way. They are too ready to measure the preacher's fidelity by the degree in which he speaks to their own immediate experience. They are earnestly engaged in particular views, feelings, trains of thought, processes of experience, which, filling their mind, seem to them all in all; and if the preacher does not touch upon these, they condemn him as dry, cold, and jejune. But they should consider, that there are other minds to be suited besides their own, and that what is so ill adapted to themselves may be precisely what is needed by others; nay, precisely what they themselves may need at another time. Instead of expressing dissatisfaction, they should rejoice that every one receives in turn a portion adapted to him, and endeavor to elicit something applicable to themselves. If they will but seek, they will often find a seasonable word when they least expect it. Let me entreat you to make this your habit. If you do not, it is plain that many Sundays will be lost to you, (for you cannot have your own case always treated,) and you will, moreover, become a fastidious and querulous hearer, discontented with yourself, and uncomfortable to others. But if you resolutely bring your mind to take an interest in whatever you hear, you will always find cause for contentment and satisfaction, if not for edification and delight.

Few things are more hostile to such attendance on preaching as shall promote religious improvement, than the habit of listening to sermons as literary or rhetorical efforts, and for the gratification of a literary taste. From the very nature of the case, it must result in constant dissatisfaction. For let it be considered how few of all the authors who have published books, are able to give this gratification; and can it, then, be expected of every preacher? How small a proportion of the thousands who have preached, have printed their sermons! and how few of these have a place among the eminent names of literature! Hence it is impossible that every preacher should, every Sunday, satisfy a man who has formed his taste on printed specimens of excellence, and who comes to gratify it at church. It is inevitable that such a one should be disappointed and displeased, far more often than he shall be tolerably gratified. Those who, on this ground, are accustomed to speak harshly of ministers, and to excite discontent in the community, would do well to reflect on the unreasonableness of the requisition, and learn that they injure themselves by ooking for what they cannot expect to find, to the neglect of that substantial good which alone is intended to be conveyed. But he who thinks only of improvement, and the religious exercise of his mind, will always find something to engage and satisfy him. Distinguished talent there may not be, nor original thought, nor striking images, nor tasteful composition, nor eloquent declamation; but Christian truth, old and familiar perhaps, but still high and important, there always will be. Dwelling upon this, excited by it to reflection, occupied in studying by its light his own character and prospects, and the perfections and purposes of God, he has no lack of interesting thought. The preacher becomes but a secondary object. His God, his duty, his salvation,—these are the topics on which his mind runs; and these he can contemplate: he will not be hindered from contemplating them, whatever may be the feebleness or deficiencies of him who ministers at the altar.

Bacon has laid down a rule for profitable reading, which ought to be sacredly applied to preaching, by those who would listen to it profitably: 'Read, not to contradict and confute, nor to believe and take for granted nor to find talk and discourse, but to weigh and consider.' What you hear from your minister, 'weigh and consider' for a religious end and a personal application. To listen as a critic, with a fastidious nicety about diction, and a captious sensibility to style, is a sure method to defeat what should be the first object with the hearer, as it is the great purpose of the speaker. For which reason, it has been remarked, we are not to be surprised that Paul, with all his energy of speech, made so few converts, and gathered no church, among the Athenians; the sensitive and intellectual taste, and love of ingenious fancies, which distinguished them, formed a habit of mind peculiarly fitted to destroy the capacity for receiving any strong and profound impressions.

In the next place, if you think that when you leave the house of God, you may discharge from your mind the thoughts and sentiments there excited; if you immediately join in frivolous society and ordinary conversation; if you occupy your time in making visits of ceremony, or in reading the Sunday newspaper and books of amusement, you can derive little advantage from the service in which you have engaged. However serious may have been your attendance, however earnest the wish for improvement, you are taking the surest method to render it all vain. The word spoken must be treasured up, the counsels of wisdom must be made to abide in the heart, the instructions and warnings of Heaven must be fixed by reflection and thought, or the impressions you have received will be transitory, and the good purposes which spring up within you will pass away like the early dew. If the preacher have presented arguments for the truth of Christianity, or for the support of any of its great doctrines, of what use has this been to you, if you shall know nothing about them to-morrow? And how can you hope to remember what is so difficult to be retained, if you take no pains to refresh your mind with it by immediate retirement and contemplation? If he have been urging you to the study of your own heart, and pointing out the sources of self-deception, and the means of preservation against the sins which easily beset you, and you have been affected and humbled, and made to resolve on greater watchfulness; of what avail will this be, if you immediately abandon yourself to frivolous topics of thought? and how are you any the better prepared for the temptations and trials of to-morrow, if you thus drive from your mind those views which were to strengthen you? Or, if he have presented to you the elevating truths respecting God, and heaven, and man's prospects of glory, and thus raised in your spirit a glow of divine love, and a sense of your exalted destiny, and you at once turn from it all to employments and thoughts which are wholly of earth; then is not that holy excitement worse than lost? have you not done something to harden your heart, and render it less capable of receiving the same impression again? For you have resisted its motions, and quenched its fire, by calling it back to this lower world when it was just beginning to delight itself in heaven.

Depend upon it, that the mere attendance upon public worship is very insufficient, without some care to fix its impressions afterward, and to recall and strengthen what you have heard and enjoyed. It is wise, therefore, to go back from church to retirement, there to think over the truths that you have heard, refresh the feelings that you have indulged, apply to your conscience the doctrine delivered, and supplicate the divine blessing. By habitually doing this, you will in time become possessed of a large fund of religious information and moral truth, which otherwise might have been lost to you; and instead of being in the condition of those, who cannot perceive that the pulpit has ever taught them any thing, you will find it a most efficient and persuasive instructer.

It is a custom, with some persons, to make a record of the discourses which they have heard, entering in a book the texts and subjects, together with a brief sketch of the train of remark. This is a very commendable and useful custom, provided it be not allowed to take off one's thoughts from the duty of self-application, and do not become a mere effort of memory and trial of skill. If this be avoided, the practice will be found useful in many respects. The exercise of writing greatly assists that of thinking, and discovers to one whether his ideas are distinct and clear. It enables and compels him to look closely at the subject, so that he cannot dismiss it with the cursory and impatient examination which he might be otherwise tempted to give it. It enables him afterwards to read, with distinctness, the impressions which he received, and to revive the purposes which he formed in consequence of them. His record becomes a spiritual monitor, reminding him, whenever he consults it, of the lessons he has learned, and the expostulations he has heard; and prompting him to a more definite comparison of his actual attainments with the standard which has been placed before him. The advantages, which may thus be derived from it, will be far more than a compensation for all the trouble attending it.

But, whether you make such memoranda or not, the practice of recalling to mind the instructions and reflections of God's house, if systematically pursued, will save you from the pain of making the complaint which we hear from so many that they cannot remember what they have heard, oftentimes not even the text; and this, too, from persons who can repeat all the particulars of a long story to which they have listened, or a longer conversation in which they have taken part. Why this difference? Partly because they attended with greater interest to the story and the conversation, partly because these are more easily remembered than a formal discourse, but principally because these are matters that they are accustomed to recall to mind and repeat, which they have not been accustomed to do in regard to sermons. The want of practice is the principal difficulty. Make it an object always to remember, and be in the habit of going over again in your mind, the principal topics, and you will not be troubled with want of memory.

I should do wrong, however, if I did not here speak a word of comfort to those humble and sincere Christians, whose advantages in early life were not such as to enable them to form any habits of intellectual exertion, and who are, in consequence, subject to a weakness of memory which they have struggled against in vain, and which is a source of constant unhappiness to them. Every thing they hear from the pulpit slips from their minds, even if it have highly moved and delighted them; and they fear that this is a sign of unprofitableness and sin. To such it may be well to recommend the reply of John Newton to one who came to him sorrowing with the same complaint. You forget, said he, what was preached to you. So, too, you forget upon what food you dined a week or a month ago; yet you are none the less sure that you received nourishment from it: and no doubt, also, that your spiritual food nourished you, though you have forgotten in what it consisted. So long as you received it with pleasure and a healthy digestion, and it has kept you a living and growing soul, it can be of no consequence whether you can particularly remember it or not.

Finally, preaching, however ineffectual it may often prove, is one of the chief means of grace, and is capable of being made, by every individual, a principal agent in his religious advancement. Let it be so to you. It will be so if you attend on it in a right spirit, and faithfully strive to gain nourishment from it.

Do not let it be your shame and guilt, that you sit year after year within hearing of the preacher's voice, and yet are none the better. Do not suffer it to be with yourself, as it is with many, that preaching grows less interesting as they advance. This, it is true, is in part owing to the nature of the mind, which finds a delight in what is new and fresh, which it does not perceive in what has been long familiar. There is a charm in listening to the word preached, when the soul is first awakened to an interest in the concerns of its salvation, and devours every sentence as a hungry man his food, which cannot be fully retained in cooler and maturer years. But if the charm be entirely gone, if the relish be altogether lost, it must be through your own fault. It must be because you have not watched over the tastes and susceptibility of your mind, but have, through neglect, suffered it to become hardened. Be but faithful to yourself, cherish your tenderness of spirit, take pains to keep alive the ardor and interest of your younger days, and you will find that your feelings will not become wholly dead to the voice of the preacher, nor will time and age be able to rob you of this source of your enjoyment. The ancient philosopher, on whom has been well bestowed the title of 'Rome's least mortal mind,' in writing beautifully of old age, tells us, that the great reason why the faculties of men are impaired in the declining years of a long life, is, that they cease to use and exercise them; and that any man, by continuing vigorously to exert them as in earlier life, may hope to retain them to the last, in something of their original power. The remark may be applied to the old age of the Christian. By faithfully watching over and exercising his feelings and emotions, he may retain them in some good degree of liveliness and vigor to the latest period. And although the zest with which he hung on the ministration of the word, in the first ardor of his youthful faith, may be gone, he will maintain a sober interest, and find a tranquil delight, suited to the serenity of his fading days, and to the peacefulness of the expectation with which he waits the summons to go home.

V. The Lord's Supper.

This interesting rite is the last in the series of Christian means which I shall mention. It is that to which the young disciple is accustomed to look forward with intense feeling, and the arrival at which constitutes an era in his progress fondly expected and fondly remembered. Sometimes it appears to be regarded too much as the limit of improvement, the goal of the course, the prize of the victory, after which the believer is to sit down and enjoy in security the attainments he has made, exempt from the necessity of further watchfulness and combat. It is owing, in no small degree, to the prevalence of this opinion, that so many make no actual or perceptible progress after their arrival at the Lord's table. They esteem it less as the means and incitement of greater improvement, than as the end and completion of the work they had undertaken; not so much a refreshment to their weakness in the trying journey of duty, as the festival which rewards its termination. Be on your guard against this erroneous feeling. Habitually remember, that your vigilance and labor are to end only at the grave; that the fight lasts as long as life; that the crown of the victor is 'laid up in heaven;' and that whatever indulgences may be granted here, they are but as encouragements to your perseverance and strengtheners to your weakness, designed to cheer and help you on your way; not seasons of repose and enjoyment, but of recollection and preparation;—so that they, in fact, form a part of that system of discipline, by which every thing below is made to try and prove the character of man.

In this light you will view the peculiar ordinance of our faith,—as a privilege and indulgence, but also as a pledge and incitement to activity in duty. From the moment that it has been your purpose to become a follower of Christ, you have looked forward to this holy feast as something which it would make you but too blest to be permitted to partake. While occupied with other means of improvement, you have still felt that there was one thing lacking, and have perhaps been stimulated to a more earnest diligence in the use of them, by the reflection that they would prepare you for this ultimate and superior enjoyment. Such is the very common experience of the growing Christian; and it is my wish to show you how that may be rendered a blessing in the enjoyment, which has been so eagerly desired in the anticipation.

Settle it distinctly in your mind, that this ordinance, so far as relates to your concern in it, has a twofold purpose; first, to express and manifest your faith in Christ, and your allegiance and attachment to him; secondly, to aid and strengthen you in a faithful adherence to his religion. That is to say, in other words, by your attendance at the Lord's table, you declare yourself to be, from principle and affection, a Christian; and you seek to revive and confirm the sentiments, purposes, and habits, which belong to that character. These are the two objects which the ordinance is intended to accomplish, and which you are to have constantly in view.

By considering the first of these, you will be enabled to decide how soon, and at what period, you ought to offer yourself for this celebration. Can you say, that you are in principle and affection a follower of Jesus

Christ? This is the question you are to put to yourself; not whether you have been such for a long time; not how great attainments you have made;—but are you such at heart, and are you resolved perseveringly to maintain this character? Look at this question. Ponder its meaning. Put it to yourself faithfully. Do nothing with haste or rashness, but proceed calmly and deliberately. Then, if you can conscientiously reply in the affirmative, if you have already showed so much constancy in your efforts, that you may rationally hope to persevere, you may make your profession before men, and take the promised blessing. Hasty minds have sometimes rushed forward too soon, and only exposed their own instability, and brought dishonor on their calling. Be not, therefore, hasty. But timid men have sometimes hesitated too long; have delayed till their ardor cooled, till they fancied they could stand and flourish without any further help, till death or age overtook them, and they were called to meet their Lord without having confessed him before men. Beware, therefore, that you delay not too long. To deliberate whether we shall observe a commandment, after our minds are impressed with a sense of the duty of doing so, is to break it. To postpone our acceptance of a privilege, when we feel that it is such, and know that it is offered to ourselves, is to refuse it, and to forego its benefits. He who believes, and is resolved to live and die in his belief, has a right to this ordinance; he is under his Master's orders to attend it; and he should reflect, that obedience, to be acceptable, should be prompt.

As soon, therefore, as your attention to religious things has sufficiently prepared and settled your mind, you will solemnly acknowledge it by this outward testimonial of faith. So far the ordinance looks to the past. It also looks to the future; and you will, secondly, as I said, use it as a salutary means of religious growth, appointed to this end, and singularly suited to accomplish it. You will regard it, and attend it, as one of the appropriate instruments by which you are to keep alive, and carry on to perfection, that principle of spiritual life, which has had birth within you, and which has made a certain progress toward maturity.

It is a means singularly fitted to accomplish this end, because it is an ordinance at once so affecting and so comprehensive:—affecting, by bringing directly before us, in one collected view, the circumstances under which it was instituted, and the purposes of Heaven with which it is connected;—the trials and sufferings of the Son of man, the meekness and sublimity of his submission, the tenderness and pathos of his last conversation and prayers, the desertion in which he was left by his disciples, the insults to which he was exposed from his enemies, the torture in which he died, submissive and forgiving; and all this, that he might seal the truth which he had taught, and provide salvation for miserable men. It is true that all this is familiar to the mind, and often brought before it in other acts of worship. But here it forms the express subject of contemplation and prayer. Here it is set before us more evidently and vividly by the circumstances, the forms, the apparatus of the occasion. It is made the special object of regard, and therefore is suited, in a peculiar manner, to affect us.

It has another advantage. It is as comprehensive as it is affecting. In its primitive intention, in its simple purpose, it is, as it was designated by our Lord himself, a commemoration of him: 'This do in remembrance of me.' And what is it to remember Jesus, rightly and effectually, but to call to mind all that he was, and did, and suffered, in his own person; and all the blessings, advantages, and hopes, which have resulted to us, and shall forever result, from his ministry and death? These are all connected together by one close and indissoluble chain. They are united, in inseparable union, with his name and memory. When we reflect on our Master, our minds cannot pause till they have gone over all his example in life and death, have recalled his character and instructions, have pondered on the excellence and beauty of his truths, the glory of his promises, the bliss of his inheritance. Thence they will pass on to survey the effects which he has already produced on the condition and character of the world, to observe the contrast of our present enviable lot with what it would have been if he had not established his reign among men, and to contemplate the spreading prospects of human felicity in the wider extension of his kingdom;—the removal of error, corruption, ignorance, and sin, and the establishment of universal truth, righteousness, knowledge, and peace. Thence they will pass on to a future world; to the unseen and unimaginable joys of a life in which purity, love, and happiness, shall be infinite in measure, and infinite in duration, and where man, made the companion of angels, freed from sin and from suffering, shall dwell in the light of God's presence without end. We shall recollect, that for all our hope of acceptance to that world, and of pardon for the sins which have made us unworthy of it; for all those gifts of light and strength which shall prepare us for it; for all the tranquillity, consolation, and support, which, in weakness, sorrow, and death, the knowledge of our immortality imparts,—for these we are indebted to Jesus Christ, without whom we should still have remained ignorant on this first of subjects, and unconsoled in the severest trials. So that, in one word, there is no topic of religion, none of thanksgiving or prayer, none of penitence, gratitude or hope, none of present or of future felicity for ourselves or for others, which is not called up to the mind by the faithful use of this simple but expressive service. As the believer sits at his Master's table, he seems to himself to be sitting in his presence; together with his image, every blessing of his faith and hope rises brightly to view; and his heart burns within him, as he contemplates the grace with which his unworthy spirit has been visited, and realizes the hope that he shall partake of the glories which his Lord revealed. As he looks unto him, 'the Author and Finisher of our faith, who, for the joy set before him, endured the cross, despising the shame,' he grows strong to do and endure likewise; animated by the hope set before him of entering into the joy to which his crucified Master has ascended.

Is it not, then, evident, that you have here a means of singular power, to keep the attention awake and the heart right; and that your spirit can hardly slumber, if you faithfully open it to the influences of this observance? Remember, however, that its value will depend on yourself, and the manner in which you engage in it. It has no mystical charm, no secret and magic power, to bless you against your will. Every thing depends on your own sincerity and devotion. Earnestly desire, and pray, and endeavor that it may do you good, and it will do you good. Go to it heedless, thoughtless, and unprepared, and it will prove to you an idle and inefficient ceremony. The great cause why so many derive no improvement from the repeated performance of the duty, is, that they attend it with inconsideration and coldness, and with little purpose or desire of being affected by it. Let your attendance be in a different state of mind. Engage resolutely in the suitable meditations; examine yourself before and after; come to the celebration with a temper prepared for worship, and leave it with one prepared for duty.

There is a peculiar feature in the mode of administering this ordinance, distinguishing it from all other acts of social worship, to which it may be well to advert. I refer to the pauses during its administration, when each worshipper is left to himself, to follow his own reflections, and make his own prayers. There are thus united in the occasion some of the advantages both of social and of private devotion. When you have been excited by the voice of the minister and of general prayer, you are permitted to retire, without interference, into your own heart, to repeat the petitions and confessions with a more close reference to your own case, and to make yourself certain that you understand and feel the service in which you are engaged. You may find a great advantage in these silent intervals. In all other instances of social worship, your attention is required, without ceasing, to some external process; and you pass on from one part of the service to another, with little opportunity to reflect, as you proceed, or to pursue the suggestions which are made, in the manner that your own peculiar condition may require. But in this, the leisure is given for thoroughly applying to your own personal state all that has met your ear, and for pouring out freely the devotional feeling which has been excited. And if there be any thing favorable to the soul, as multitudes of devout persons have insisted, in occasions for contemplative worship in the presence of other men, then, in this respect, the

Lord's supper may claim a superiority over every other season of social devotion.

Many persons, I am aware, find it difficult so to control their minds as to render these silent moments profitable. But to such persons the very difficulty becomes a useful discipline, and the occasion should be valued for the sake of it. To aid them in the use of it, and to prevent its running to waste in miserable listlessness and idle rovings of the mind, it might be well that they should have with them some suitable little book of meditations and reflections, which they may quietly consult in their seats as guides to thought and devotion.

In a word, prepare your mind beforehand, be faithful during the celebration, review it when it is past; and you will never have reason to complain of its inefficacy as a means of religious improvement. You may not enjoy high and mystical raptures; you may be sometimes overtaken with languor and coldness; but as long as, in sincerity, and from motives of duty, you present yourself in this way before the Lord, you will find that there is refreshment and encouragement in the act

You will have in it satisfaction, if not ecstasy; and will never doubt that something of the steadfastness of your principle, and of the vigor of your hope, is owing to this affectionate application of the life, example and sacrifice of the Saviour, in the way of his appointment.

CHAPTER V.

THE RELIGIOUS DISCIPLINE OF LIFE.

NEXT to the means to be employed in the promotion of personal religion, we must attend to the oversight and direction of the character in general. The means of which we have taken notice, consist of a series of special and stated exercises, whose object is to prepare us for the right conduct of actual life; and they may be compared to the daily drill of the soldier, by which he is made ready for the field. Watchfulness and self-discipline belong to all times and occasions, and may be compared to the actual use which the soldier makes of his preparation in the camp and the field. The Christian is engaged occasionally in prayer, meditation, study, and the communion; he must watch and govern himself always. To the former duties he devotes certain appropriate seasons; the latter belong to every season and all hours. The former constitute his preparation for the

Christian life; the latter constitute its pervad ing spirit. No punctuality or fidelity in the former proves a man to be religious without the latter. And therefore, having stated the manner in which these means are to be used, it is necessary for us to go on and show how they are to affect the whole conduct of life, and make it an exercise of perpetual self-discipline.

Why you are to be always watchful over yourself, is easily perceived. In this world of sensible objects and temporal pursuits, you are constantly exposed to have your thoughts absorbed by surrounding things, and withdrawn from the spiritual objects to which they should be primarily attached. You are incited to forget them, to slight them, to counteract them. The engagements, the anxiety, hurry, and pleasures of life, thrust them from your thoughts; and desires, propensities, passions, are excited quite inconsistent with the calm and heavenward affections of Christ. All these tendencies in your situation are to be resisted. You are to be ever on the alert, that they may not lead you into any course of thought or of action at variance with the principles to which you are pledged as a believer in Jesus Christ, and which form your delight in your hours of devotional enjoyment. Such inconsistency may be sometimes witnessed. But what can be more melancholy than to see a rational being, deeply convinced of the truths of religion, in his sober hours of thought dwelling on them with fond and delighted contemplation, excited by them to a devout ardor of communion with God, and sometimes to a glow of holy rapture which seems to belong to a superior nature;—and then sinking into worldliness, governing himself in ordinary life by selfish maxims of temporal interest, obeying the passions and propensities of his animal being, and, in a word, living precisely as he would do, did he believe that there is nothing higher or better than this poor life? I ask, what can be more sad or pitiable than such a spectacle? Let it be your earnest care to guard against so deplorable an inconsistency. Now, while your mind is warm with its early interest in divine things,—now, while they press upon you in all their freshness,—now, take heed that you do not concentrate that interest, and use all its strength, in the luxury of devout musing or the excitements of study and devotion; but carry it into your whole life; let it be always present to you in all you do, in all you say; let it form your habitual state of feeling, your customary frame of mind and temper. Make it your constant study that nothing shall be inconsistent with it, but every thing partake of its power. This is the watchfulness in which you must live. This is the purpose for which you must exercise over yourself an unremitting and ever-wakeful discipline; seeing to it, like some magistrate over a city, or some commander over an army, that all your thoughts, dispositions, words and actions be subject to the law of God, and the principles of the Christian faith.

Thus it is plain, that your chief business, as well as your great trial, in forming a Christian character, lies in the ordinary tenor of life. The WORLD is the theatre on which you are to prove yourself a Christian. It is in the occurrences of every day, in the relations of every hour, in your affairs, in your family, in your conversation with those around you, in your treatment of them, and your reception of their treatment;—it is in these that you are to cultivate and perfect the character of a child of God. It is in these that your passions are exercised, and your government of them proved; in these that your command over that unruly member, the tongue, is made known; in these that temptations to wrong doing and evil speaking beset you, and that you are to apply your religious principle in resisting them. In these it is, consequently, that you discover whether your principle is real and genuine, or whether it lies only in feeling and in words. In the quiet of your chamber, in the devout solitude of your closet, when the world is shut out, and your solemnized spirit feels itself alone with God, you may be so exalted by communion with Heaven, and by meditation on heavenly truth, that all things earthly shall seem worthless and paltry, and every desire be set upon things above. How often, at such times, does it appear as if the world had no longer any charms, as if its pleasures and pomp could never again entice or delight us! Our souls are above them. We have no more relish for them than have the angels. And if this were all which is required of us, if nothing opposed to this delightful frame of mind were ever to cross our path, the Christian prize would be already won. But, alas! in the closet, and in the third heaven of contemplation, we can live but a small portion of the time. We must come down from the mount. We must enter the crowd and distractions of common life. We must engage in common and secular affairs. And there, how much do we encounter that is opposed to the calm and serene spirit of our contemplative hours! how much to irritate and disturb our quiet self-possession! how much to drive from our thoughts the subjects on which we have been musing! how much to revive the relish for transient pleasures and worldly enjoyments, and a love for the things which minister gratification to pride and to the senses! In the midst of these things, dangerous, enticing, seductive, you are to live and walk unchanged, unseduced, undefiled; your heart true to its Master, your spirit firm in its allegiance to God, and your soul as truly devout and humble as when worshipping at the altar. Is this easy? I will not ask; but is it not your great, your paramount, trial? Is it not here, that the very battle of your soul's salvation is to be fought? Is not this, as I said, the very field of actual and decisive war, the very seat of the fearful and final campaign? And the prayers and studies, and observances of your more special devotion, are they not the buckling on of the armor, and the refreshing and preparing of the soul for its real combat?

You perceive, then, how the Christian life must consist in watchfulness and self-discipline; how it must be your great business to keep a faithful guard over yourself, that, both in mind and conduct, nothing may exist contrary to the spirit and precepts of Jesus Christ.

First of all, this guard is to be placed upon the Mind. It is an intellectual, internal, spiritual discipline; the oversight and management of the thoughts and affections.

There is a superficial religion, not unpopular in the world, which is limited to the outward conduct and the external relations of life; which is made to consist exclusively in rectitude of behavior and uprightness of dealing. Into this error you are not likely to fall, if you learn your religion from the New Testament; and I should not have thought it needful to warn you against it, had it not been so prevalent. Nothing but its commonness could render it credible, that men, who possess the Scriptures, and fancy they understand them, or who are simply capable of observation on the nature of man and of happiness, should persuade themselves that the character which God demands and will bless, is independent of the state of the mind and the frame of the affections. Is it not the mind which constitutes the man? Is it not the mind which gives its moral complexion to the conduct? Is it not certain, that the same conduct which we applaud as indicating an upright character, we should disapprove and condemn, on discovering that it proceeded from base and improper motives? So that even *men* judge of character rather by the principle which actuates, than by the actions themselves. How much more completely would this be the case, if, instead of being obliged to infer the principle from the act, they could discern the principle itself as it lies in the mind of the agent! Who, in that case, would ever judge a man by his actions alone? Who would not always decide respecting his character from the principles and motives which guided him,—his thoughts, dispositions, and habitual temper? And thus it is that the Deity judges and decides. He looks not on the outward appearance, but on the heart. Consequently, how obvious is the position, that, in seeking the Christian character, the first and most diligent watch must be placed over the inner man! 'Keep thy HEART with all diligence; for out of it are the issues of life.'

This implies several things. First, a careful guard over the Thoughts. It is in the heedless disregard of the thoughts that corruption often takes its rise. They are suffered to wander without restraint, to attach themselves without check to any objects which attract the senses, or are suggested in conversation, and to rove uncontrolled from one end of the world to another. How many hours are thus wasted in unprofitable musing, which leaves no impression behind! How much of life is made an absolute blank! Worse still, how often do sinful fancies, sensual images, unlawful desires, take advantag of this negligence to insinuate themselves into the mind, and make to themselves a home there, polluting the chambers of the soul, and rendering purity unwelcome! This is the beginning of evil with many a one, who, from this want of vigilance over the course of his thoughts, has surrendered himself to frivolity and sensuality, without being aware that he was in peril. Thoughtlessness, mere thoughtlessness, has left the door open to sin, and the same thoughtlessness prevents the detection of the intruder.

You may fancy that your present preference for profitable subjects of thought, is such that you are in no danger from this source. But beware of trusting to any present disposition. If you become confident, you will fall; and the rather, because the beginning of this peril is so subtle and sly. Believe that the danger is real and imminent, or it is scarcely possible that you should not suffer from it. You may not, indeed, fall a victim to irregular desires and hurtful immoralities; but the habit of unwatched thought will weaken your control over your mind, will diminish your power of self-government, and rob you of that vigorous self-possession, alive to every occasion, and prompt at every call, which forms the decision of character that ought to belong to him who professes to follow the energetic principles of Christian morality. So that, if you would be saved from an unbecoming weakness of mind, and its possible, not to say probable, consequences, ungoverned desires and passions, keep a guard upon your thoughts. Let your morning and evening prayer be, that you may live thoughtfully. And when, in the business of the day, your hands are occupied, but your mind free to think, keep yourself attentive to your thoughts. Inquire frequently how they are engaged. Direct them to useful and innocent subjects. Think over the books you have been reading; rehearse to yourself the knowledge you have gained; call up the sermons you have heard; repeat the passages of scripture you know. By methods like these, take care that even your empty hours minister to your improvement. Paley has truly observed, that every man has some favorite subject, to which his mind spontaneously turns at every interval of leisure; and that with the devout man the subject is God. Hence the watching over your thoughts furnishes you with a ready test of your religious condition; it exposes to you the first and faintest symptoms of religious decline, and enables you to apply an immediate remedy.

If the thoughts, which may be expressed in words, are to be thus guarded, the Temper and Feelings, which are often so indefinable in language, require a no less anxious guardianship. In the perplexities and trials of daily life, in the conflict with the various tempers and frequently perverse dispositions of those around us, in the little crosses, the petty disappointments, the trifling ills which are our perpetual lot, we are exposed to lose that calm equanimity of mind which the Christian should habitually possess. We are liable to be ruffled and irritated, and to feel and display another spirit than that gentleness which 'bears all things and is not easily provoked.' The selfishness of some, the obstinacy of others, the pride of our neighbor, the heedlessness of our children, and the unfaithfulness of our dependents, tire our patience, and disturb our self-possession; while bodily infirmity and disordered nerves magnify insignificant inconveniences into serious evils, and irritate to peevishness and discontent the temper which duty calls to cheerfulness and submission. Some are blessed with a native quietness of temperament which hardly feels these hourly vexations. But of some they form the great trial, and peculiar cross; they can bear any thing better. And to all persons they constitute an exposure full of hazard, and demanding cautious vigilance. The very spirit and essential traits of the Christian character require watchfulness against them, and imply conquest over them. The humility, meekness, forbearance, gentleness, and love of peace; the long-suffering, the patience, the serenity, which form so lovely a combination, which portray a character that no one can fail to admire and love;—these are to be maintained only by much and persevering watchfulness.

Without this, the most equable disposition by nature may become irritable and unhappy. With it, under the authority and guidance of Christian faith, the most unfortunate natural temper is subdued to the gentleness of the lamb. Without it, the internal condition of man is restless, rebellious, full of wretchedness, having no peace in itself, and enjoying nothing around. With it, the aspect of the world becomes changed; every thing is bearable, if not pleasant; the sweet light which beams within, shines on all without, making pleasant the aspect of all men, and smoothing the roughnesses of all affairs. Who does not know how much the events of life take their hue from the state of the disposition? To the proud, suspicious, and jealous, every man seems an intruder, every gesture an insult, and every event a cause of vexation and wrath. To the self-governed and amiable, every thing is tolerable, and he feels nothing of the inconveniences which make the misery of the other. One's happiness, therefore, as well as duty, requires this control of the disposition. And when the Saviour pronounced his benediction on the pure, peaceful, humble-minded, and meek, he taught, not only the great requisite of his spiritual kingdom, but the great secret of human felicity.

When the frame of your mind is thus a constant care, you will find little difficulty in the control of the Appetites. These things are connected together; and, an ascendency over the former being secured, the subjection of the latter easily follows. But take good heed that it does follow. Do not be thoughtless about it, because you fancy that it will of course accompany a regulated mind. Otherwise it is here that corruption may begin. The enemy will enter at any place, however improbable, which shall be left unguarded. And it only needs that the body become disordered through the immoderate indulgence of the appetites, to raise a rebellion throughout the whole moral system; or, to speak more plainly, this indulgence will create cloudiness of mind, indisposition to thought, activity, and duty, irritability of temper, sluggishness of devotional feeling, and at length a general spiritual lethargy. There can be little doubt, that much of our dullness of apprehension and deadness of feeling on spiritual topics, as well as our strange sensibility to minor trials, is owing to a derangement of the animal economy, which is again owing to want of moderation in gratifying our animal desires.

Hence there was some reason in the abstinence and fastings of religious men in ancient times; and if we valued sufficiently, what they perhaps valued superstitiously,—serenity and brightness of mind, an equal temper, and a perpetual aptitude for spiritual contemplation,—we should imitate them more, if not in their fastings, yet certainly in their temperance. At any rate, 'let your moderation be known unto all men.' For temperance is not only the observance of an express injunction, but is essential to that quietness and self-control which should mark the religious character.

The next exercise of self-discipline will be in Conversation. Conversation, while it is a chief source of improvement and pleasure, is also a scene of peculiar trial, and the occasion of much sin. One might suppose that few persons ever dream that they are accountable for what passes in conversation, although there is no point of ordinary life which Jesus and the Apostles have more frequently and sternly put under the control of religious principle. Their language is strikingly urgent on this head; and yet, so little scrupulousness is there among men, even religious men, that it would seem as if they felt ashamed to be careful in their talk. A thoroughly well-governed speech is so rare, that we still say, in the words of James, 'If any man offend not in word, the same is a *perfect* man.'

Do not allow yourself to be off your guard in this respect. Make it a part of your business, by a cautious prudence, to have your speech consistent with the rest of your character. Do not flatter yourself that your thoughts are under due control, your desires properly regulated, or your dispositions subject as they should be to Christian principle, if your intercourse with others consists mainly of frivolous gossip, impertinent anecdotes, speculations on the character and affairs of your neighbors, the repetition of former conversations, or a discussion of the current petty scandal of society; much less, if you allow yourself in careless exaggeration on all these points, and that grievous inattention to exact truth which is apt to attend the statements of those whose conversation is made up of these materials. Give no countenance to this lamentable departure from charity and veracity, which it is mortifying to observe commonly marks the every-day gossip of the world. Let precision in every statement distinguish what you say, remembering that a little lie, or a little unchar itableness, is no better than a little theft. Be slow to speak those reports to another's disadvantage, which find so ready a circulation and are so eagerly believed, though every day's experience shows us that a large proportion of them are unfounded and false. In a word, be convinced that levity, uncharitableness, and falsehood, are as truly immoral and irreligious in the common intercourse of life, as on its more solemn occasions; that idle and injurious words make a part of man's responsible character, as really as blasphemy and idolatry; and that 'if any man seem to be religious, and bridle not his tongue, that man's religion is vain.'

'A word spoken in season, how good it is!' Why should you not do all in your power to elevate the tone of conversation, and render the intercourse of man with man more rational and profitable? Let your example of cheerful, innocent, blameless words, in which neither folly nor austerity shall find place, exhibit the uprightness and purity of a mind controlled by habitual principle, and be a recommendation of the religion you profess. Let the authority of that faith to which you subject every other department of your character, be extended to those moments, not the least important, in which you exercise the peculiar capacity of a rational being in the interchange of thought. Never let it be said of your tongue, which Watts has truly called 'the glory of our frame,' that with it you bless God, and at the same time make its habitual carelessness a curse to men, who are formed in the similitude of God.

The influence of the principle which rules within, should thus be seen in all your deportment and intercourse, on every occasion and in every relation. Your outward life should be but the manifestation and expression of the temper which prevails within, the acting-out of the sentiments which abide there; so that all who see you may understand, without your saying it in words, how supreme with you is the authority of conscience, how reverent your attachment to truth, how sacred your adherence to duty; how full of good-will to men, and how devoutly submissive to God, the habitual tenor of your mind. Your spontaneous, unconstrained action, flowing without effort from your feelings, amid the events of every day, should be the unavoidable expression of a spirit imbued with high and heavenward desires; so that, as in the case of the Apostles, those who saw them 'took knowledge of them that they had been with Jesus,' it may in like manner be obvious that you have learned of that holy Teacher. And this may be without any obtrusive display on your part, without asking for observation, without either saying or hinting, 'Come, see my zeal for the Lord.' The reign of a good principle in the soul carries its own evidence in the life, just as that of a good government is visible on the face of society. A man of a disinterested and pious mind bears the signature of it in his whole deportment. His Lord's mark is on his forehead. We may say of his inward principle, which an Apostle has called 'Christ formed within us,' as was said of Christ himself during his beneficent ministry;—It 'cannot be hid.' There is an atmosphere of excellence about such a man, which gives savor of his goodness to all who approach, and through which the internal light of his soul beams out upon all observers. Consequently, if you allow yourself in a deportment inconsistent with Christian uprightness, propriety, and charity, you are guilty of bringing contradiction and disgrace on the principles which you profess; you expose yourself to the charge of hypocritically maintaining truths to which you do not conform yourself. You dishonor your religion by causing it to appear unequal to that dominion over the human character which it claims to exert. All men know that, if 'the salvation reigned within,' it would regulate the movements of the life as surely as the internal motions of the watch are indicated on its face; if the hands point wrong, they know, without looking further, that there is disorder within. That disorder they will attribute either to the incapacity of the principle, or to your unfaithfulness in applying it. But, what is of far greater importance, the holy and unerring judgment of God will ascribe it to the single cause of your own unfaithfulness; and for all your wanderings from Christian constancy, and all the consequent dishonor to the Christian name, you must bear the shame and reproach in the final day of account.

You perceive how urgent is the call for perpetual watchfulness and rigid self-discipline. It is not easy, with much intentional guard over yourself, to keep the spirit habitually right in this giddy and tempting world; and it is equally difficult to maintain a perfect coincidence between the principle within and the deportment of daily life. Oftentimes, in the emergencies and hurry of business, pleasure, and society, where many things concur to drown the voice of the spirit within, we find the lower propensities of our nature gaining an ascendency, and the law in our members rising in rebellion against the law in our mind. 'The things that we would, we do not, and the things that we would not, those we do;' and sense and passion triumph for the moment over reason and faith. 'The flesh lusteth against the spirit, and the spirit against the flesh, and these are contrary the one to the other.' And how shall we gain the victory in this perpetual contest? 'Through our Lord Jesus Christ,' says the Apostle; and the means thereto are found in his injunction, 'Watch and pray, that ye enter not into temptation.' Vigilance over every hour and in every engagement, carrying into them the shield of faith and the whole armor of God; and prayer, without ceasing, that your soul may be strong to wield them;—these will secure to you the victory. Sometimes you will find yourself in perplexities and straits, sometimes faltering and irresolute; but never forsaken or cast down, never exposed to temptation which you are unable to bear, or from which there is no way of escape. You may 'do all things through Christ who strengtheneth you.'

I have thus spoken of that religious discipline of daily life, in which the Christian character is formed and tried. It will be sufficient to add, in conclusion, that your great concern must be with two things,—your principles and your habits.

First, you must constantly have an eye to your Principles. Take care that they be kept pure, and that you abide by them. They have been well compared to the compass of the ship, on which if the helmsman keeps a faithful eye, and resolutely steers by it in spite of the opposition of winds and waves, he will find the way to his port; but by heedless inattention to it, he is sure to go astray, and be blown whither he would not. Be assured that it is only by adherence to principle, in resolute defiance of inclination, opposition, present interest, and worldly solicitation, that you can ensure the steady progress of your soul, and its final arrival in heaven. Neglect it, and you are at the mercy of circumstances, tossed helpless on the waters of chance, exposed to the buffetings of temptation without the power of resistance, and a sure prey of the destroyer. You must find your safety in the strength of your principle; and that strength lies in the original power of conscience, and the added authority of the divine word. Herein is the 'still small voice' of Heaven; and he that will 'cover his face' from the world, and obediently listen to it, may become morally omnipotent.

Secondly, have an eye to your Habits. Add to the authority of principle the vigor and steadfastness of confirmed habit, and your religious character becomes almost impregnable to assault. It is in no danger of overthrow, except from the most cunning assailants in a season of your most culpable negligence. What wisdom and kindness has the Creator displayed in our constitution, that we are able to rear around our virtue the strong bulwark of habit! It is a defence of the weakest spirit against the strongest trial. Through the power of habits early formed, how many have stood in exposed places, and been unaffected by solicitations to sin, beneath which others have fallen, who trusted to their good purposes, but who had never confirmed and invigorated them in action! How often, for example, has the young man from a retired situation,—educated in the bosom of a virtuous family, and under the eye of a watchful father, thence sent forth to the new scenes of a city life, under the protection of good principles and a sincere purpose to do well,—been found weak and wanting in the exposure; and been carried away headlong by the tide of temptation, because his early habits were suited only for seclusion, and his principles were guarded by none which could secure them against the novel assaults that were made upon them! While, on the other hand, young men brought up in the midst of these solicitations to sin, with far less inculcation of principle, are oftentimes enabled, through the mere strength which habit imparts, to resist them all, and live in the midst of them as if they were not.

It cannot be necessary to multiply examples. You well know what a slave man is to his habitual indulgences, and how the customary routine of his life and methods of employment tyrannize over him, and how frequently one strives in vain to free himself from their dominion. The old proverb is every day verified before you, of the skin of the Ethiopian and the spots of the leopard. But, if thus powerful for evil, habit is no less powerful for good. If in some cases it be stronger than principle, and defy all the expostulations of religion, even when the miserable man is convinced that his safety lies in breaking from it; then, when enlisted as the ally of principle, when coupled with faith, and made the fellow-worker of piety, how unspeakable may be its aid toward the security and permanence of virtue!

Take heed therefore to your habits. Allow yourself to form none but such as are innocent, and such as may help your efforts to do well. In the arrangement of your business, in the methods of your household and family, in the disposal of your time, in the choice, seasons, and mode of your recreation, in your love of company, and your selection of books,—in these preserve a simple and blameless taste. Do not allow any of them to be such as shall offer an obstacle to serious thought, and induce a state of feeling indisposed to religious exercises. Especially do not allow them so to enter the frame and texture of your life, that every effort of virtue and devotion shall be a pitched battle with some cherished inclination, or sturdy habit. This is to increase most unwisely and needlessly the trials and perils of a religious course. It is to raise up for yourself obstacles and difficulties beyond those which properly belong to your situation. Rather, therefore, arrange every thing in your customary pursuits and indulgences to favor the grand end of your being; so that every act of piety and faith shall be coincident with it; so that little or no effort shall be required to maintain the steady order of daily duty; and, instead of an opposition, a struggle, a contest, whenever principle asserts its claims, you shall find the ready consent and hearty coöperation of all the habitual preferences, tastes, and occupations, of your life. He in whom this is so, is the happy man. He is the consistent man. He is the man to be congratulated, to be admired, to be imitated. Universal harmony reigns within him; no oppositions, no jarring contentions, mar his peace. With him, the flesh and the spirit are no longer contrary the one to the other. His duty and his inclination are one. There is no dispute between what he ought to do, and what he wishes to do. But, with one consenting voice, heart and life move on harmoniously, accustomed to and loving the same things. To him the yoke is indeed easy, and the burden light. To him heaven is already begun; and when at last he shall be welcomed to the joy of his Lord, it will be to a joy which his regulated spirit has already tasted in the labors and pleasures of obedience below.

PROGRESS

OF THE

CHRISTIAN LIFE

ADVERTISEMENT.

At the period when Mr. Ware's health began irrecoverably to fail, and just before he was obliged to give up all occupation, he was devoting his hours of leisure to the preparation of a sequel to his work on the Formation of the Christian Character, which he designed to entitle "Progress of the Christian Life." Several chapters only were finished. They are too valuable to be lost, and are here published in the hope that they may be useful. The reader will form by them an idea of what the sequel would have been if its author had lived to finish it.

C. R.

AUTHOR'S PREFACE.

The following pages are designed as a sequel to the little work on the Formation of the Christian Character, and are supposed to be addressed to the same persons. When one has adopted the Christian faith as his rule of life, and begun in earnest his religious existence, it is still but the commencement of a career in which an indefinite progress is to be made, and which is to continue forever. As long as man is imperfect, there is room for improvement. As long as he is in the flesh, there is occasion for watchfulness and struggling against temptation. There is need that his principles become more and more fixed, his conscience more and more enlightened and controlling, his passions more thoroughly obedient to the law of righteousness, and his whole temper and demeanor more steadfastly conformed to the example of Christ. In a word, he is to *grow* in grace. Advancement is his duty, perfection his aim.

It is with regard to this duty of religious progress that I propose to offer a few hints. There are some errors respecting it prevalent among believers, which I would first attempt to rectify; and then I would explain its true nature and character, remove discouragements, and show the means and steps by which it should proceed, and how actual success is to be ascertained.

CONTENTS.

N. B. The following titles of additional chapters or sections are given in Mr. Ware's manuscript:—

Hinderances. How Progress manifests itself, and is to be ascertained. Progress in Knowledge, in Self-government, in Spirituality of Temper, in Conscientiousness, in Disinterestedness, in Power to resist Temptation. In what sense Perfection is to be expected, &c. &c.

PROGRESS

OF THE

CHRISTIAN LIFE.

CHAPTER I.

ERRORS RESPECTING THE DUTY OF RELIGIOUS PROGRESS NOTICED AND CORRECTED — ESPECIALLY THE ERROR THAT THE CHRISTIAN LIFE, HAVING BEEN BEGUN, IS ACCOMPLISHED.

NOTHING can be plainer than that the Christian character is a thing to be *acquired* and to be *improved;* yet it is evident that many do not so regard it. If we may judge from their conduct, the number is not small of those who esteem it something which belongs to them just as the body does, and to be kept alive and in health just like that, by living along from day to day, as the circumstances of each day may suggest, but not to be the subject of any special regard. But as to being every day better than the day before, as to being more humble and charitable this year than they were last, it does not enter their mind, it makes no part of their plan. They have been Christians, they say, as long as they can remember; they always believed in the gospel, and meant to do their duty. But they do not know more about the history and foundation, the nature and purposes, of their religion, nor are they in any respect more devoted. Indeed, when one thinks seriously on the subject, it is a matter of amazement to him to observe how stationary good men are, and how quietly they content themselves with being so.

It is not so in other matters. We look around us on the community, and we see it in a state of commotion and advancement. Its prosperity is a wonder to us, and that prosperity is progress. Every one is pushing forward. Every one is eager and panting for success. Our young men rise step by step; they are discontented if they find it otherwise. Those who began life with nothing are seen in a few years comfortably living with a family around them, — then entering a larger dwelling, supporting a more extensive establishment, and in various expenses evincing the advancement they have made. This is common. But meantime — even if they account themselves Christians, and remember that they have an eternity as well as a family to provide for — they have not dreamed of exhibiting any proportionate advancement of character; it has not occurred to them that their piety should have grown with their estate; that their charities should have been as much greater than formerly as their income has become larger; that, as they have been rising in the world, they should have risen also toward heaven. In the eye of the world, they are better dressed and better lodged, and they move in a more fashionable and intellectual circle; but in the eye of God, in their preparation for heaven, they are just where they were. They have contrived to give the soul just food enough to keep it of the same stature — not considering that it was to grow as well as the body — not considering, indeed, that this eager attention to worldly good, and rapid growth in earthly prosperity, have very probably stunted the growth of their characters.

How salutary might it prove to every one whom Providence has blessed with an increase of goods, if, at every enlargement of his style of living, he should devote one day to searching into his spiritual progress, and resolve never to erect a new house, or introduce a higher indulgence to his domestic economy, until he could honestly say, that he was as much improved in character as in fortune!

But, alas! this is far from being the way of the world. They are satisfied to seem to themselves no worse than they were; — if they deeply examined themselves, they might discover that they are, in fact, much worse.

Amid this universal and earnest struggle for the outside life, the inner life is neglected; and very good men are entirely content to be no better, who could ill brook to be no richer.

Certainly this indicates a false idea of the true object of life, and a very imperfect acquaintance with that religion which they profess to have taken for their guide. I do not treat the question in its reference to mere men of the world. On their principles they are right. With a worldly man, character is of very little consequence. If he be not dishonest, so as to be in danger of the law, — if he keep a decent reputation for fairness and the social virtues, so as not to hinder his success by becoming obnoxious to others, — what more can he need? His business is to make his fortune and enjoy himself more and more every year; and this he can do perfectly well without being a better man. This, therefore, need be no part of his concern. But with those who profess to look beyond the world, to whom the favor of God is of some consequence, as well as the opinion of men, and who soberly believe that virtue is better than wealth, — with such as I am now addressing, — it should be the chief concern. Is it possible that they can have adopted Christ as their Master, and taken his religion as the great guide and blessing of their souls, knowing themselves to be immortal, and yet be satisfied to see their earthly condition prosperous while there are no signs of their souls' prosperity? Surely the last must be their great anxiety and care, or they are strangely false to their principles. There is no incompatibility between the two; both may advance together; but to strive only for the earthly is treachery to their principles. Alas! then, how many such traitors are there!

But there is another class. All do not, even in this prosperous community, succeed in their anxious efforts to advance themselves in the world. Many make no progress. They gain no wealth, they never enlarge their means of living and enjoyment, they live on as they began. Perhaps they are content with their lot. Many, it is well known, are perfectly so. They acquiesce in the allotment of Providence, and quietly sit down where God has appointed them. But many more have tried to rise, and in vain. Are they satisfied then? Do they content themselves? Do they make no effort further? Do they feel no regret, mortification, and longing? Surely not so. Waking and dreaming, they are haunted by the restless desire and the unquenched hope of reinstating their fortunes. And yet, though they know that their souls are equally far from prosperity, and that they have made no improvement in religious knowledge and virtue, it does not make them uneasy; they are perfectly willing it should be so. They are quite content to find themselves no better Christians; but they cannot bear to find themselves no more wealthy.

It was a beautiful wish of the disciple whom Jesus loved, when writing to a dear friend, "that he might be in health and prosper *even as his soul prospered.*" I fear it would be thought a strange wish now, even amongst those who esteem themselves very good disciples. They would not understand how the prosperity of the soul is the first thing. Many, it is to be feared, do not even place it second. Business, money-getting, is first; their family, second; religion is postponed to the third place, at least, and very little honored in that, if we may judge by its advancement in comparison with that of the other two.

There are undoubtedly other classes to be

found, besides those whom I have now named. They need not be described. They leave but a small number to be found scattered among us, here and there, as we look around, whose business, aim, object, is the growth of their character, who live for the sake of the soul, and who evidently, markedly, become better men as they advance in life. We would not be cynical in our estimate, but none can look around on society, Christian society, — recollecting with what capacities for goodness men have been endowed, and what inducements to progress toward perfection are always before them, — without a feeling of amazement, mortification, and alarm, at observing how few are growing, or striving to grow, in the virtues of the Christian life. So rare are such instances, that they are looked on, and spoken of, as bright exceptions; and a measure of goodness which ought to be that of every man, nay, which all acknowledge to be still far short of what the Christian should be, is described, praised, and held forth to imitation as something extraordinary — as, indeed, beyond what men in general are expected to attain. "We are not to *expect* to find others as good as he."

This defective tone and condition of society is unquestionably a great hinderance to those who are young in religion. It presents to them, on their first entrance to a new principle, instead of examples that stimulate to effort and excellence, and raise still higher their impressions of the purity and spirituality of Christian attainment, specimens of lagging, sluggish, moderate virtue, which countenance them in the most indolent exertions for improvement. As they look forward with the glowing mind of youth and the first beatings of awakened faith, the Christian life looks to them not only all light and glorious, but of a strict and holy austerity, and a scrupulous purity which has no part or lot with the ordinary follies of humanity — elevated above the world by a taste which has no pleasure in its perishing pursuits, and a habit of exalted contemplation which dwells amid things unseen and eternal. They begin the race, therefore, with feelings of high aspiration. They take their place among the disciples with a romantic and earnest expectation of finding in those privileged persons something, they know not what, of a celestial temper and beauty: they expect to be incited, cheered, instructed, by the very contact, and to find in the atmosphere in which they dwell the radiance and perfume of heaven. And if they could find it so, they would keep alive their own ardor, they would persevere to realize their own exalted conceptions. But they find it otherwise. The image which they had conceived in their own minds of what the Christian man ought to be — an image whose features were all drawn from the life and teaching of the Great Master — is not at all realized in the world. Nobody acts up to it. Nobody seems to have it in mind. The common standard is wholly below it; and these young beginners find themselves alone, with an idea and purpose of a perfection which the more experienced smile upon as the extravagant dream of youth, which a few more days will show them to be impracticable in such a world as this. Thus the actual state of religious feeling chills the early blossoms of their religious characters: they find that much less than they had imagined is thought sufficient by the older and wiser disciples, who must know much better than themselves; that it is by no means requisite to follow Christ so nearly, or worship God so exclusively, as they had fancied; they discover that, in fact, they have made as great attainments already as the world would bear; to proceed further would be only to become singular: so they change their purpose, and remain where they are; unwilling to be better than others; satisfied with a measure which seems to satisfy others, and glad to learn that the great work they had undertaken is so early completed. And thus each generation does its utmost to repress the aspiration of the next, and to keep down the standard of virtuous attainment.

So powerful is the example of the society around us, and such the influence of prevailing notions to modify our own, that few have courage or perseverance to follow the inward suggestion which urges them to rise higher. So that a distinguished minister gave it as his earnest advice to a young friend, not to allow himself to be ordained as pastor of any church in which the standard of life was not very strict and high; because, as he urged, all experience shows how almost impossible it is for a young minister to escape conforming himself to the sentiment around him, and being shaped more or less by the popular mould. If it be thus to be apprehended in the case of one all whose *temporal* interests urge him, no less than his *eternal*, to rise to the MARK, how much more must it be so with ordinary men, who are less protected by the circumstances of their position, and the daily duties of their calling!

It is, therefore, evidently, one of the first duties of the young Christian to settle it in his mind that he has only commenced a work which is to be going on as long as he shall exist. Every thing in the example and experience of others around him proves how necessary this is, for it proves how easily he may be made to forget it.

There are also some mistaken notions respecting religion itself which may lead to the same error; the idea, namely, which so readily finds a welcome in the mind which is glowing with the first happiness of its early faith, that its glow cannot fade away; that things will always appear to the soul just as they do at that divine moment; that the new taste is fixed, and cannot be changed; that it will take care of itself. Hazardous and unfounded as such a feeling is, it is yet very natural. It belongs to all strong emotion to have faith in its own perpetuity. The affections always are confident that they never shall change; and we always fancy that the grief, or love, or indignation, which fills our bosoms now, can never fade from them. When, therefore, we are awake to the vivid consciousness of our spiritual relations, and are overwhelmed with those various and mingling emotions that take possession of the excited spirit, and blend there in all that is awful, tender, joyous, and serene — when we are confident that now, at last, we are tasting the highest gratification of which human nature is capable, that now, at last, we are in the state in which man ought to be, — a state in which things appear as they are, in their true relations and proportions, and the common things of the world take rank among the insignificant and uninteresting, — we cannot doubt that these, the truest, will be the lasting feelings; we cannot conceive it possible that any thing on earth should ever have charm enough to entice from this state; that any of the things which we now know to be inferior should ever be able to withdraw us from what we now know to be supreme. This is the hearty, honest, deeply-seated conviction within us. This is the conviction which occasions the well-known confidence and presumption of young converts, which prompts to their proverbial forwardness — a confidence and forwardness often attributed to unworthy motives, and spoken of to their discredit. It may not be creditable to them; yet it argues nothing worse, perhaps, than self-ignorance. They do not know the evanescent character of the feelings, the deceitfulness of the heart; therefore they give way to it; they trust themselves; they spread all their sails to the wind, as if it would never change; they fancy themselves established, and act warmly and boldly, as if established. But this glow is necessarily transient, like all vehement feeling; and when it has passed away, they have no abiding principle of life to take its place and keep the work in progress. Other feelings rise up in the midst of the world; the brightness of the spiritual light fades from before the eye of the soul, and there is no advancement to a higher perfection.

Let no one, therefore, from the strength and security of his first affections, allow himself to rest, as if the work were done. It is but begun. Let him settle within himself, deeply and sternly, the persuasion that it is to be going on while life lasts. For want of this it is that the love of so many has waxed cold, and that so many who put their hand to the plough have turned back. If you would persevere, you must understand, at the outset, the necessity of perseverance. You must start with the conviction that you begin a perpetual progress.

For which reason, instead of looking at the state of society, instead of conforming yourself to the model of those with whom you live, study into the nature and capacity of your soul, your destiny, and your responsibility; imbue your mind with the spirit of your immortal faith, and the influence of the character of your holy Master; and from the promptings of a soul thus filled and kindled, act out Christianity for yourself; — not as others do, nor as others expect you to do, but as this state of mind impels you. There is no true and safe course but to be obedient to these suggestions of a mind which has faithfully studied for itself into the doctrine and temper of the divine life. These suggestions are to it as the instinct of its immortal nature — as unerring, as safe, as the instincts of the lower orders of beings. Man's bodily instincts are as nothing, for his bodily interests are of little moment, and in pursuing them he has no need of an infallible guide. But the interests of his undying soul are of infinite consequence: in his search for them he needs an infallible guide; and that guide he has in the promptings of his own mind, whenever he has cultivated it with the deep study of truth and faith, and steeped it by faithful contemplation in the secrets of divine love and infinite purity, and brought it into intimate communion with the Holy Spirit of God. If you have truly acquainted yourself with your Master and his revelation, — if you have entered into their spirit with your whole soul, — then act yourself, freely, boldly, and you will not know what it is to stop short. This very action will be progress.

CHAPTER II.

ERRORS NOTICED AND CORRECTED — ESPECIALLY THE ERROR THAT THE CHRISTIAN LIFE IS NOT TO BE TAKEN UP EXPRESSLY — IS NOT TO HAVE A MARKED COMMENCEMENT.

Besides the causes of error which are hinted at in the preceding chapter, there are others still more worthy of consideration. Of these I do not know that there is any more common or more detrimental than that which is the subject of this chapter. It is an error which arises naturally from the circumstances of birth and education in a Christian land, and from the idea that under such circumstances the Christian character grows up of course, just as the social does, and perhaps as part of the social. It differs from that before mentioned in this, that, while that supposed the Christian character something to be formed by a certain process in a certain time, — to be done by the job and finished at once, — this supposes that it is never any thing to be taken up as a distinct subject of attention, or to be made an express concern; but is to be left to take care of itself, under those influences to which all are subjected, and beneath which it will grow up spontaneously. This is a common error; it infects the great mass of nominal Christians; it deceives and paralyzes even conscientious men, and keeps them from all progress by persuading them that the soul will grow of itself, as the body does.

This error is so widely connected with misapprehensions respecting the origin and nature of the religious life, that it cannot be fully developed without a wide discussion. But it is of less importance thoroughly to do this, than to exhibit the error itself. It has no doubt been fostered by the manner in which the axiom has been received, that all safe progress is gradual, that whatever is violent and sudden is unnatural and unsafe — an axiom true in itself, when rightly understood, but very falsely applied in the present instance. Is not the progress of the day gradual, it is asked, and the progress of the seasons imperceptible? Does not the seed germinate and spring forth without our being able to detect or trace it; growing night and day, we know not how; first the blade, then the ear, and then the full corn in the ear? Are not all the beneficent operations of Providence and nature thus?—never rapid, vehement, instantaneous, but always gentle, quiet, gradual? And, satisfied with this analogy, we sit down to wait the advancement of our character, just as we wait the progress of the season; as if we had only to sit and wait; to do nothing to hasten or retard it; as if its course was onward as inevitably as fate. We do not perceive that we advance; but no matter: who sees the sun advance on the dial-plate? We have no consciousness of being in motion; but, then, who sees the motion of the planets, or the increase of the blade of corn? We are making no efforts: certainly not; for a growth, to be healthy, must not be forced. Who would have the sickly and short-lived produce of the hotbed?

But even if we chose to follow strictly the analogy between the insensible universe and the living moral soul, this mode of reasoning is unjustifiable. If we do not see the day come forward with our eyes, we perceive clearly, after an interval, that it has come forward; and though our keenest sight does not detect the growth of the plant, we yet do see that it has grown; and we should be extremely unhappy if the opening dawn should become stationary, or the grain and fruit should pause in the process of ripening. But those of whom I speak feel no uneasiness at the perception that their characters have become stationary; they are not troubled when, at the greatest intervals, they still find that they have gained nothing. All is made quiet in their conscience at once by the sovereign pacifier, "O, we are not to expect great results: improvement must be gradual; the more gradual, the more sure."

Has not this lamentable result been encouraged in many minds by the expression of a very eminent writer of great influence? —"that our Christian congregations contain two classes: to the one must be preached conversion, to the other improvement" — an altogether just remark, which commends itself at once to every man's approbation. But how easily misapplied! Every one, on hearing it, bethinks himself, of which class is he? "I do not need conversion; I have been religiously educated; always attended church, always read my Bible, always accounted myself a Christian; I only need improvement. My case, then, is safe; I am on the right side, and of course it will be for my interest to improve; in fact, considering the advantages amidst which I live, I cannot fail to improve: 'tis not in the nature of man to live under such excellent preaching and with such facilities for reading and worship, and yet not improve." Thus perfectly satisfied with his situation and with himself, he folds his arms and does nothing. The current floats him along, and he does not dream that it can be to any other than the true haven.

If I should address such persons, I would ask them if they do not presume too much, when they thus take it for granted that they do not need conversion. Does it by any means follow, because they have been educated under Christian institutions, that they have availed themselves of them, and become

Christians? Because they have been taught to read the Bible from their childhood, does it follow that the spirit of that holy book has formed their characters? Certainly this cannot be pretended. One may be brought up in the very recesses of the sanctuary, and yet be as corrupt as an abandoned heathen; may believe that Christianity is from heaven, as the Hindoo believes that his ancestral faith is divine, and be in heart addicted to all that is unchristian. History and observation tell of but too many who have contended for the faith, and yet who had checked no desire, controlled no passion, at its bidding. It is not, therefore, impossible that many decent men may have been brought up amongst us to honor Christianity, who yet are far from being imbued with its spirit; that many may have a respect for its precepts and a jealous attachment to its forms, and yet be governed at heart by principles which it would disapprove. Doubtless there are many such: they are willing to count themselves its friends; they are proud to number themselves among its supporters; and, being thus Christians by birth, claim the right to be esteemed

Christians indeed. But in order to be Christians indeed, they must be religious men; and religious men they are not: they need to be converted to the influence of the faith they honor; from the worldliness which governs them, to the personal experience of the power of the truth, which as yet is a dead letter to them. They think they need only to go on: alas! they have not yet begun. They have the very first step to take. They have the commencement to make.

Is it not to be feared that many are living and dying amongst us in this very condition? Is there not a quieting and deceptive influence in much of what passes for religious sentiment amongst us, producing the feeling that we have all begun — we have all entered the path of life — we have only to go on? But it is not true that all have begun. How, then, can it be otherwise than dangerous to entreat all to go on? How can they advance if they have not commenced? There can be no true and satisfactory progress unless we are sure that we have made a beginning, and a right beginning.

Now, the great error is, that men are con-

tent without any *proof* that they have made a beginning. They are willing to assume this important and all-essential fact as a thing of course.

They were born in a Christian land; they believe Christianity divine; they are pretty good men; they trust, through God's mercy, they shall be saved. But this does not prove that they have in any proper sense commenced the Christian life. What are their ruling principles? On what rest their affections? Where are their motives, desires, and to what are their self-sacrifices offered? Get an honest reply to these questions, and you find that *the world* still rules them. A faith in things spiritual, and a supreme surrender to God, they as yet know not. *They have a beginning yet to make.*

I hold it to be clear that no man can have done so important a thing as to resolutely take up the Christian law for his guide, without a consciousness afterwards that he has at some time distinctly done so. It is a very momentous act in a man's life when he assumes the obligations and responsibilities of the word of Christ, and says, "For this

Master I live and die." He must know that he has done it. It is not a thing to be taken for granted — to be supposed. The bearings of this faith on his daily life in a thousand ways — its applications to his temper, his thoughts, his will, his habits of living and speech — are too direct and palpable to leave any doubt on the subject. The struggle between this spirit of allegiance to conscience and faith, and the fleshly appetites and worldly principles; the trials, and falls, and recoveries, and shame, and joy, and all the various tumults of mind and heart, which the Christian pilgrimage implies, are all too distinct, too deeply felt, too strongly marked, to be forgotten, or to allow room for conjecture, supposition, or any testimony but the heart's own consciousness. Many, very many, have been so situated in early life, and have been so formed by influences exclusively of the world, that they can at no time come to a Christian life without most conspicuous and absolute change — a disruption of former ties, a more or less painful abandonment of former habits, a strange and entire alteration of the favorite and ruling desires. Educated as most persons are, it is impossible that they should otherwise arrive at the Christian life; and this change is an era to be remembered. It leaves deep marks on the history. And as for others, who have been favored with a more propitious lot, and whose minds have received the sanctifying influence of truth from the cradle, drinking in divine knowledge with their daily discipline, and imbued with the temper of Heaven through the power of the society and teaching of their early guides, — they, too, cannot have confirmed their early impressions excepting through efforts and struggles; they must evidently *know;* it cannot be left to them to take for granted. They may have the most infallible proof that they have actually made a beginning.

But as for the great class of those who can produce neither of these proofs, how can they proceed? They are grossly self-deceived. Their trust and hope are altogether without foundation.

No wonder that they are content without progress. After assuming, without evidence, that they are Christians, it is a small thing to add the assumption that they move while they stand still.

Here, therefore, I propose to my readers, that they institute a solemn and thorough self-examination. Let each inquire and know whether he is one of this very extensive class, who thus easily imagine themselves to be something when they are nothing. If he has never yet doubted on the subject, nor rigorously inquired, he has reason for apprehension. Let him dwell no longer in uncertainty, or content himself with conjecture. Let him ascertain whether he has actually made a religious beginning. If not, let him waste no time in studying how to make *advancement.* He has an earlier and more important work — to remove away all the heavy rubbish which, through his self-deception and long blindness, has been accumulating about him, and lay in earnest the foundation of a hearty faith, and a holy, heavenly character. If he is not sure that he has already begun the Christian life, let him begin now, to-day, with a prayerful determination, with a devoted purpose, with a heartfelt self-consecration to God, and Christ, and duty. Let him leave this great matter no longer in suspense, this most momentous question no longer open, but let him bring his real character and his hidden motives into the light — the clear light of truth — by taking devoutly and resolutely the first grand step, by performing the initiatory act of intelligently, distinctly, and with a single heart, dedicating himself to the service of his heavenly Master.

CHAPTER III.

ERRORS NOTICED AND CORRECTED — ESPECIALLY THE ERROR OF THOSE WHO FANCY THAT THE CHRISTIAN LIFE MAY BE SUSTAINED WITHOUT THE USE OF MEANS.

I HAVE endeavored to expose the mistake of those who dream that the religious life has no beginning. I now turn to those who fancy that it may be sustained and supported without the use of means.

In stating their error thus, there is absurdity on its very face, so great that it may be supposed impossible for any one to maintain such a position. And perhaps to the full extent none will venture to maintain it in *terms*, though we certainly hear language which very nearly approaches the statement I have made, and daily witness conduct which is consistent with no other principle than that which such a statement involves. In fact, it is the tendency of the speculations and the practice of the day to make light of forms, to undervalue modes of operation, to speak of times, persons, places, ceremonies, as unessential, material, instrumental, — as crutches for the lame, leading-strings for the weak, guides for babes, — quite necessary to those who are so far wedded to the body that it clogs and impedes their minds, but wholly unnecessary to the soul itself; in fact, as badges of an inferior condition, as marks of spiritual backwardness, as the remnants of an earthly dispensation, and relics of the infancy of our race, which are fast becoming unnecessary in this enlightened age, and which the truly enlightened had best dispense with at once.

There is a good deal of loose thinking and talking of this sort. It is founded on a misapprehension of the real nature of the advancement of man in the present world; as if cultivation and religion were making an actual change, not in his condition and advantages, but his very nature; relieving him of his dependence on the body, the senses, and the material world. Whereas, evidently, he must retain still his connection with them, his relation to them, and must be affected by them in his desires, appetites, habits, enjoyments, character — must act through them, and be acted on by them; and so long as this is so, it is perfectly impossible that he should be able to maintain a purely spiritual existence, or to advance his spiritual character, without aid from abroad. While this connection with the outward world perpetually operates on him to affect his temper and distract his affections, it is necessary to counteract it by agents and contrivances which also operate outwardly. While, every day, appetite must be indulged at stated hours, business done, and exciting thoughts, interests, and passions absorb his mind, he must every day have stated means of neutralizing their engrossing and infecting power, or they will obtain the mastery.

How it may be when the soul shall be separated from its present connection with the body, we do not know. Perhaps then it may go on a course of holy progress without external aid, or stated help; though the Scriptures give no representations which warrant us to decide peremptorily that it is so. Certainly it is not so now; and they who fancy it to be so, are taking the sure method to dwarf their own stature and chill their devout affections.

There is, undoubtedly, a distinction to be made between religion and the means of religion — a distinction, the want of attention to which has led to great abuses, and been the parent of fanaticism and superstition. Forms and ceremonies have been exaggerated into the essentials of faith; opinions have been made to take the place of character, and days and observances have usurped the respect which should have been paid to righteousness and true piety. In order to avoid this error of times past, it has become a favorite notion with many, that religion only, should have attention and honor — pure, unmixed, unaccompanied religion. They are to become religious; that is the great end; they are to form perfect characters. Religion does not consist in saying one's prayers, attending church, observing the Sabbath, sitting at the Lord's table, reading the Bible: these things are not religion. One may do all these, and yet not be religious — men have done all, scrupulously, and yet been reprobates. These are but the means; and if one be but a religious man at heart, it is of no consequence whether he scrupulously observe these means or not. Indeed, he had best avoid any approach to a superstitious regard for them; it would belittle him; it is best to have a great deal of freedom. One should not be a slave to certain hours; he can pray at any time; a prayer is just as acceptable at the work-bench, and in the street, as at the altar; and every day ought to be a Sabbath; one day has no more real sacredness than another. There is great danger of mistaking the means for the end; we will pursue the end only.

Common as something like this may be in the thoughts of many and the practice of more, it is yet wholly indefensible as a matter of reasoning, and utterly ruinous when applied to practice. Here and there a man may be found who can live on these principles uninjured; but they are extraordinary men; the great majority would infallibly be destroyed by them.

They lead to a disregard of religious services, which will extend, in too many instances, to a disregard of religion itself, and will often inevitably cause the Christian character to fall into decay, because the props which are necessary to support it are removed. So serious an evil deserves to be carefully considered. There can be little hope of general advancement or great attainment in religion, when such opinions are prevalent.

Let it be considered, therefore, that although, abstractly and strictly speaking, there may be an essential distinction between an end to be gained and the means by which it is to be gained, for all practical purposes there is no difference whatever. If the result be desirable, and can be attained only through a certain process, that process is of precisely the same consequence as the result. If the affair be one of duty and obligation, the obligation to perform the process is as absolutely binding as the obligation to effect the result. If I desire to hold an eminent rank in society, if I wish to be a promoter of human good in an important profession, it is just as important that I should pass through the discipline of that preparatory education which fits for the profession, as it is that I should enter on that profession. My usefulness and eminence depend equally upon both. It is not enough, in order to the arrival of a steamship at a distant city, that the crew be at their posts, the engineer at his wheel, and the machinery all in beautiful order; the boiler must be filled and the fire kindled; and he would be a stupid commander who should slight these because they are only means — who should say that his object was to arrive at the city, and he was not to be busying himself about these little preliminaries to progress. Yet it would be hard to understand how there is any less stupidity in those who fancy themselves able to arrive at heaven, while they slight the appointed means of proceeding thither as wholly secondary affairs. I ask, "Are you a student of the Scriptures? Do you daily and statedly pray? Are you fond of frequenting occasions of religious worship?" Your answer is, "O, no! religion does not consist in these things. I am only careful about the great end; that is all which I need to regard." That is to say, so long as you are resolved to arrive safely at the end of your journey, it is of no consequence whether the water, and the wood, and the fire, be applied to the boiler or not! "But," I add, "one would imagine that your own feelings would prompt you to join in these religious observances and acts — that your own religious state of mind and heart would lead you to take pleasure in them." "Why, yes, *sometimes*, now and then; and *then* it is well enough to attend and use them. But unless one happens to be *disposed* to engage in them, it is not worth while to do so. It is only the great end which I am anxious about." "And thus," I reply, "caring only for the *accomplishment* of your voyage, you have no rule but your *inclinations* to decide when you shall *feed the fire* which is to carry you on."

One would be glad to ask of the great men who have blessed the world with their light and action in any department of usefulness — especially one would like to ask of the apostles and reformers — how this doctrine would have operated in their case, and where the world would have been if they had been beguiled by it — if Paul, instead of his journeyings and toils that he might preach the gospel, and establish and organize churches, and so save men's souls and extend the kingdom of Christ in the world, had thought within himself, "Preaching, and worship, and the Christian community, are only the means of salvation; they are but secondary things in comparison with salvation: salvation, salvation, that is the great, prime, all-absorbing consideration; and why should I be wearing out my life on the mere means?"—or if Luther and the other men that have moved the world with their doctrine had sat silent on the happy suggestion that *preaching is not religion* — RELIGION is the great thing to be regarded? And yet, where is the man who can show that it would have been more absurd in *them* thus to have forsaken the preaching of the gospel, and the gathering of assemblies, than it is in any private man to forsake the hearing of the word on the same pretence?

And yet there are men who practise and defend this unspeakable absurdity! They think themselves good Christians, and yet waste the hours of the Sabbath, are slack in their attendance on public worship, almost strangers to the Bible, without worship in their families, and without stated prayer in their closets; and, if you expostulate with them, very soberly reply, that these things do not constitute religion; they care only for religion itself. And thus there is not one of the means appointed for and essential to religious establishment and growth which is not put by on this plea.

It is evident enough, I think, that these means, if not parts of religion, are yet essential to it. But I go still farther. I ask if it be so unquestionable, as appears to be taken for granted, that they are *not parts of religion.* Is it so clear that the reading of the Scriptures, acts of devotion, and attendance on the ordinances, are not essentially, and in their own nature, parts of religion as well as means? Let us look at this. What is religion? Strictly speaking, it is something invisible, intangible, immaterial — which has no shape, and is not cognizable by any human sense. Practically speaking, it is a certain character — that state of mind, heart, and character, which become the relation in which a man stands to God. Now, I ask, what is that state of mind, heart, or character, without the expression of it? Is not the expression of it, properly speaking, a part of it? Can we say that there is character where there is no manifestation of it? If we were consulting philosophical exactness of terms perhaps this might be disputed; but so far as regards real life and the common judgment of men, it is doubtless correct. We know nothing of real benevolence of heart, if in no way manifested — nothing of uprightness and strength of character — nothing of intellectual power — except so far as *expressed;* and this expression is always regarded as part of the character itself; it is the character acting.

Now, religion is a certain state of mind, heart, and character; but if there be no manifestation of this state in action, neither the individual himself nor other men could be assured of its existence and reality. But what are the expressions, what the manifestations, of religion? The most natural, perhaps the most spontaneous, the most indubitable, is prayer. It is the *expression* of the religious heart to its God. It is the language of the devout mind. It is the action of the pious spirit. I cannot conceive, therefore, that any one should esteem prayer simply a *means* of religion. It is a part of religion. It is an inalienable concomitant. And it is represented, throughout the Scriptures, more frequently as an essential act of religion, — inseparable from and inherent in a devout character, — than as a means of increasing the devotional temper, or of spiritual improvement.

The same is true concerning the Christian ordinances. To express faith and newness of spirit by baptism, and to commune with the Savior at his table, are in themselves religious actions. To read the Scriptures, and devoutly meditate on the truth of God, and worship in his house, and listen to the preaching of his word, are religious acts, expressions of a religious character, no less than means of increasing in Christian knowledge and holiness.

It is, therefore, far from true that, in neglecting religious observances, we merely postpone the means to the end. They constitute, in their very nature, parts of that which we seek to achieve. They are natural *expressions, manifestations*, of the religious character; and one can hardly be authorized in imagining himself to possess that character, if it do not thus display itself.

If it be still said that one may make his selection from these means, and use those which best suit his own case and satisfy his own want, it may be replied, Undoubtedly he may find greater edification in some than in others, and to such he may with peculiar interest apply. But he can hardly think himself at liberty to *slight any*, so long as all have been appointed by God, and are regarded as part of man's service to him; so long, too, as each of them is only another mode of giving expression to that spirit which he professes to desire to cultivate, and which he ought to find pleasure in expressing.

If these things be so, every man's duty becomes plain, and he can live in neglect of it only at the hazard of a great absurdity, which casts his soul into fearful peril.

CHAPTER IV.

THE YOUNG CHRISTIAN PUT ON HIS GUARD AGAINST THE HINDERANCE TO PROGRESS WHICH ARISES FROM DISAPPOINTMENT RESPECTING THE ENJOYMENT OF A RELIGIOUS LIFE.

AMONG the hinderances against which the young Christian may need to be put on his guard, we may mention, next, that arising from false expectations respecting the enjoyment of a religious life. The opening views of a religious existence are like those of youth, bright with vague anticipations of the future, full of gay dreams, romantic and visionary expectations. It is the youth of the soul, excited, ardent, confident, and painting the future in colors too uniformly gorgeous to be true. Not that any extravagance of expectation can exceed the actual happiness which the Christian realizes in his established faith. Young Christians do not, for they cannot, expect too much; but they expect — as the Scripture says "they ask — *amiss.*" They err as to the nature more than as to the degree of enjoyment. They look for it in excitement, in strong emotion, in ecstasy, in rapture. They expect to be forever in the same glowing frame of bliss in which they are now, while the subject is all new and their feelings all fresh. The scales have just fallen from their eyes, the light has broken in upon their souls for the first time, and the scene that bursts upon their view is that of Elysium. They have no idea that familiarity can ever render it less beautiful, or dull in any degree the emotion with which they gaze upon it. But it is a universal and inexorable law of nature, that familiarity tames the passionateness with which any object is regarded. The excitement of feeling goes down. The exaltation and frenzy of the mind subside. The pleasure may continue, but the rapture ceases.

He, therefore, who proceeds to cultivate his religious nature under the expectation that it is to yield him a perpetual, sensible joy, is sure to be disappointed. It is not the nature of the mind to be capable of perpetual, unintermitted joy. In all cases in which the mind is wrought up to a high pitch of excitement, one of two consequences always results — either it becomes weary, and the interest of the subject is worn out by the intenseness of the action, — and this often happens in religion, where a most passionate devotion for a season ends in coldness, indifference, and worldliness, — or else, the excitement being modified and controlled by reason and principle, the mind settles down into a quiet, steadfast, gentle, and equable condition, without ecstasy, but full of content. And this, too, is what we see in daily examples of the judicious and confirmed believers.

Many are made greatly unhappy, and fall into grievous despondency, for want of duly considering this. They find erelong that their frame of mind sinks. Not only have they no rapture, but they perceive with horror that occasionally even a lethargy of feeling comes over them, as if they had fairly exhausted the excitability of their mind. They read and pray with a calmness which frightens them — a calmness they in vain try to agitate; and whereas they were shortly before lifted to the third heavens with delight, they now stand unmoved, as if the very pulse of celestial life had stopped. The contrast appals them. They fancy themselves deserted of God and all goodness. They feel themselves abandoned and lost, and are ready to sink in consternation and despair. They had imagined, in their hours of exalted musing, that the love of the world was subdued; that the power of its fascination was gone; that its follies and lusts, its pride and pleasures, having been seen once in their true light, could never have charms for them again; and that the sinful feelings they had formerly excited could not be excited by them again. But, as they again move about in the actual scenes of the world, they find it far otherwise. The desires and appetites which they supposed to be dead, were only sleeping, and they suddenly wake. The passions and selfishness which they supposed subdued spring up vigorously, and would break their chains, and clamor for indulgence, as before, and, perhaps, in some unguarded moment, seize on their gratification. All this astonishes and alarms them. They were not prepared for it. It is wholly unexpected. They find themselves deceived. They know not how to meet it. They are miserable. Their life is wholly a different one from that which they proposed to themselves — a life of watching, self-denial, and anxiety, when they had been looking for nothing but peace and joy. They are disheartened, and perhaps abandon the path which promised them pleasantness and peace, but has yielded them weariness and pain.

It becomes important, therefore, that the beginner should understand the nature both of Christian duty and of Christian happiness, that he may count the cost before he begins, and not fail through false and unreasonable expectations.

Let him consider, then, that Christian duty is conformity to a law, and Christian happiness the result of that conformity. This law governs the affections, as well as the conduct; determines the whole state of mind and feeling, as well as of life; and it is only when mind and feeling are conformed to this law that the man is in the way of Christian duty, — only then, therefore, that he is to expect happiness. And what happiness? That which belongs to the consciousness of having done duty; that which grows out of and appertains to the state of mind which is attained; — and that will be, of course, satisfaction, contentment, rather than ecstasy. The consciousness of being right, the assurance of the favor of God, — these, being abiding and habitual impressions on the mind, are likely to produce a calm peace, rather than a tumultuous delight.

Then it is to be considered, further, that religion operates on the human mind upon similar principles with other subjects, and follows the laws and constitution of human nature. If, then, in respect to the question before us, the analogy of the other affections shows the same result, we ought to be satisfied. And undoubtedly it is so. The religious affections are kindred to all the affections. That love which is the essence of religion is the same love which exhibits itself in the various relations of man, and is the source of the purest and strongest joys of earth, as it is to be of those of heaven. How intense and fervent the love of a mother for her child! What sacrifices will she make for it, what toils endure, and how readily does her heart flutter and her eye overflow! Yet there are times when that strong affection seems dead in her bosom, and we have often heard her say that it seemed to her as if she had no feeling, as if she were an unnatural creature, from whom all natural affection had departed. Yet, meantime, unexcited as she is, she goes resolutely on, discharging her maternal duties, till some occasion calls forth again the floods of tenderness. She did not blame herself—we did not blame her—for that habitual tranquillity of feeling, for that temporary coldness;—far from it. The cares of a large family never could go on, if the parent were agitated always with the intense feeling toward all the children which is the real measure of her love for each; and we know that she gives as genuine proof of her affection where the work she does for them takes her thoughts away from them, when she forgets them for a season, because she is so busy for their good, as when she overwhelms them with caresses and tears.

So, too, the father of the household. He leaves them in the morning, is absorbed with the toilsome cares of his business, and may not be distinctly conscious of a thought or emotion going back to them during the day. Is it proved, then, that he does not love them? Time was, when the image of her who is now the mother of his children haunted him like a dream, mingled with all his thoughts, could not be, would not be, banished from his mind: it was like a light about him wherever he went, and a bliss in his thoughts however he was employed; and thus his love was one perpetual living rapture. Because it is so no longer, does he therefore love her the less? Nay, he loves her the more, — with a sober, steadfast, habitual confidence and affection, which has lost its passion, but has become an essential portion of his being, — intrudes on him less, but in its calmness and quietness blesses him more. It is only the idle dream of romance which expects the rapture of the lover to be perpetuated in the sober certainty of waking bliss which makes the happiness of home. And so of all the affections. The religious affections go by the same law. When newly awakened and fixed on the great realities of God and eternity, they engross, and agitate, and absorb the soul; there is no room for any other thought, affection, or care; these fill and consume the whole being. But by-and-by the heart settles into a state of tranquillity; and the man, occupied in obedience and duty, is excited less, and walks with his faith as an old and familiar friend.

Let it, then, be no discouragement to the religious aspirant, that familiarity with his new life has abstracted something from the keen relish it had at first. Let him learn to find an equal satisfaction in the moderate and unexciting life of tranquil duty, that he at first found in the strong emotions of the mind. Acceptance with God depends on the heart being right with him; and as you do not judge of the rightness of your child's affection toward yourself and the other children by its vehemence of expression, by its being easily called out in tears and vented in outcries, but rather by its steady and unobtrusive watchfulness for your wishes, and carefulness not to offend, and fidelity, and kindness,–

so believe that the great Father judges of you, and approves you none the less because the strength of emotion with which you first came to him has subsided into an equable confidence and uniform obedience.

And here I cannot refrain from saying a few words in relation to another source of discouragement, which often operates in connection with that, to the consideration of which this chapter is especially devoted.

The Christian is very frequently disheartened, not only at finding less excitement and rapturous enjoyment in the religious life than he expected, but also at not discovering such obvious marks of progress in the advancing stages as at the commencement. But it is a very important truth for him who is going forward in the Christian life to remember, that the growth of character follows, in many respects, the analogy of all other growth. In its beginnings it is more perceptible; its progress in its first stages is more striking: an extraordinary difference is in a very short time noticed, after a man has positively changed from worldliness to religion. But the succeeding steps become by-and-by less perceptible; and though actual, perhaps equal progress may be made in a more advanced state of the Christian course, yet the work may seem to be almost stationary. An illustration of this may be found in the different appearances of motion in the rising and the meridian sun; the former seeming to advance with rapidity, the latter hardly to move. Or take, for comparison, a work of art, a painting. The artist takes a blank and unmeaning canvass. He sketches the outlines of his beautiful subject. A very short time suffices to exhibit great progress. The whole form and features come rapidly into view. But, as he approaches towards the finishing of his work, he labors the more delicate parts — he retouches, refines, perfects; but it all makes little show: in truth, there may be more and more careful study, and anxious toil, and the highest efforts of his genius, and yet the amount of labor and thought, and the degree of improvement, be perceptible to none but a most observing and practised eye. So it is with the Christian character the nearer it approaches to perfection: there may be great watchfulness, laborious self-discipline, toil for advancement, and a perpetual addition of those delicate strokes, those hues and shades of spiritual beauty, by which perfection is attained; but no change shows itself, meanwhile, to the common observer; the Christian seems to others precisely where he was a month ago, and he himself may be dissatisfied at not perceiving any obvious marks of growth corresponding with his arduous labors.

Let the Christian, then, not be deceived. Let him be sure that he judges himself by a right standard. It is true that he ought not to be too easily satisfied of his improvement; but neither ought he to be discouraged through an irrational regard and judgment of his moral condition. When the oak was just springing from the ground, and rearing its stem in the increase of its first tender season, its growth of but twelve inches above the soil, whereon nothing but decayed leaves was manifest before, appeared conspicuous and considerable; but now that it has waved its branches in the sunshine and winds of threescore summers, and sheltered two generations of men with its beneficent shadow, and nurtured innumerable tribes of living creatures in its kindly arms, it may add the same measure of increase in a year to each of its hundred gigantic limbs, with no perceptible enlargement; its real growth has been a hundred-fold what it was when most conspicuous to men, but no one observes or appreciates it. So it is with the Christian character: the more advanced its stages, the nearer it attains to perfection, its actual improvement, though greater than in the beginning, may nevertheless be less perceptible.

In view of the discouragements alluded to in this chapter, and of all others that might be enumerated, I would say to him who has really entered on a religious life, "You have taken the only rational course, the only safe course, the only truly happy course: persevere unto the end; run with patience the race that is set before you; fight the good fight, keep the faith, lay hold on eternal life. Light is sown for the righteous, and gladness for the upright in heart."

CHAPTER V.

CONSIDERATIONS DESIGNED TO ASSIST THE CHRISTIAN IN THE SUCCESSFUL USE OF THE MEANS AND METHODS OF RELIGIOUS PROGRESS.

In order to the successful use of the means of religious progress, so that they shall truly operate to a religious growth, it is essential so to employ them as to create an equal, healthy development of the character in all its parts, so as to avoid the inconsistency and distortion which are the consequence of too exclusive devotion to some, and the comparative neglect of others. A perfectly well proportioned religious character is rarely to be found; but for that very reason it should be the more anxiously desired.

Character is constituted of the state of the mind and affections, and the habits of life. These ought all to be in harmony with each other, — directed by the same principles, exhibiting the same features, wearing the same complexion. If they disagree, there is a painful discordance perceived; something is wrong; there is neglect of duty, blame somewhere.

Now, the means of cultivating and perfecting the right state of mind and affections are, primarily, meditation and prayer, and those mental exercises of contemplation, self-examination and study, by which the soul is directly wrought upon and raised to a spiritual fervor. Thus it approaches to God, cherishes holy and benevolent desires, and comes to love and enjoy the things that are unseen and eternal. And when, from the seasons of contemplation and thought, the man goes into the scenes of active life, he carries with him this propensity to goodness, these desires to do well. He goes with a mind imbued with the sentiment of devotion, and the spirit of dutifulness.

Thus far, well. But the character is not yet complete: the habits of his active life make part of it. And what are they? Do they correspond with this internal frame? Are they in harmony with these principles and sentiments?

We are ready at first to ask, "How can they be otherwise?" But we are soon reminded that it is often even so. It is common to witness lamentable inconsistencies between the feelings and the conduct. Some men appear to live two lives. They seem to have two souls. In private thought and in familiar converse they are devout men. Their sensibilities are quick; their emotions are strong; their sense of God lively; and they greatly enjoy their seasons of devotion and reading. But in the routine of life they are worldly, grasping, self-indulgent, devoted to gain, neglectful of trusts and duties, and far inferior to many who have no religious sensibility, who find little enjoyment in retirement and reflection, but who have accustomed themselves to the most scrupulous fidelity in every passing hour of social life.

It is to be with you, therefore, a matter of study and effort to carry the sentiment of the closet into action. The life of contemplation must not contradict the life of action. It is but partially that character is formed which is formed only by thinking, musing, and purposing. It wants the completeness of active habits. It wants the test which is to be found only in life. It wants the principle of growth which can be found only in action. And this is what is particularly to be considered in this connection — *action is an essential and all-important means of religious growth;* so much so, that even the contemplative graces, the virtues of the mind, true affection, exalted principle, benevolent dispositions, — which we are ready to believe thrive best in solitude; to cultivate which, multitudes have shut themselves out from the world, that they might have nothing to do but to meditate, read, and pray, — even these fail of their true perfection unless quickened and ripened by action. For consider a moment. When the mind is thus excited and glowing with divine truth and virtuous thoughts, is it not all so much impulse to do something? Does not the desire spring up spontaneously, prompting to act, — that is, to express itself? But there is no opportunity to act, and the impulse is denied. It is excited again, and again denied. What is the consequence? It is enfeebled. It becomes less and less strong. It fades and dies from the soul.

Generous impulses, not acted upon, perish; the soul loses its sensibility, becomes callous. It has long been a familiar accusation against a certain sort of sentimental reading, that it tends to consume and waste the sympathies, and paralyze the affections, by highly exciting them, but allows them not expression in action, awakening the impulse, but refusing to gratify it. It is equally the case with all religious affections. And it is easy to understand how they who trust to them as if sufficient, and take no pains to carry them out in act, may come to exhibit two distinct characters — elevated thought and glowing feeling, but selfish indolence of life and cold inactivity.

Consider, therefore, that action is an essential means of religious growth. Follow out the highest impulses of your mind. Obey the suggestions of your conscience. Never deny the religious promptings of your feelings. Then you will establish the dominion of principle, the supremacy of conscience. Then all good feelings, having received their natural and intended gratification, will be encouraged and strengthened, because they have had their legitimate exercise.

Remarks to the same purpose may be made respecting the relation which subsists between *principle* and *habit.* Habit is a thing of tremendous power: it is sometimes omnipotent in man; and it is of the greatest consequence that its energies be as much as possible, and as easily as possible, secured on the side of virtue. It may be the greatest helper or the greatest hinderance to improvement. It was intended to be the former; and yet to how many, through life, does it prove the latter! In how many men does virtue make toilsome growth, because clogged, thwarted, depressed, by unfortunate habits! — habits formed in early life, established in the flesh, rooted in the affections, woven into the daily routine of conduct, till they become a part of the very nature; and the poor wretch whom they enthral is bound down to a miserable insignificance of character, and yet is wholly unaware of their deleterious predominance. They are habits, for example, of luxurious living, of perpetual personal indulgence, of slothfulness, of mental inaction; they are around him like a heavy and deadening atmosphere, through which his spirit has to make its way upward, and by which its flight is perpetually retarded. It has always been so, and he does not know it; or, if he knows it, how difficult to enforce the remedy! But in most instances he has no conception of the true nature of the evil which hinders him; is not, perhaps, even aware of his grievous want of alacrity and progress — like the perpetual invalid, who has borne about with him from time immemorial a seated disorder which enfeebles him, but has no violent symptoms, and who still engages in all the general duties of life, without the vigor and delight that other men know, but with all the vigor and delight that he ever knew, and therefore without any consciousness of the extent of his own deficiency; and who never can be conscious how far he is below the vigor and spirits of other men, except by being delivered from his ailment and made like other men. So is it with him whose moral power is palsied by the unpropitious habits I have referred to: he never can know the degree in which they are an injury to him, until, having thrown them off, he sees how rapidly he rises without them.

There is the greatest reason, then, that one should strictly examine himself in this respect; that he may not be depressed forever by circumstances in his modes of life, of whose injurious influence he is ignorant, and which he might counteract if he knew them.

But could he counteract them? It will not do to answer, No; and yet the difficulty is in many cases so all but insuperable, that we are ready to understand in their literal sense the words of the prophet, and believe that the undertaking is as desperately hopeless as that of changing the leopard's spots, and the Ethiopian's skin. To take the most familiar example: there is the drunkard. He continues such against his own will, in spite of his own resolutions, in contradiction to his own interest, tears, professions, purposes, principles. His bad habit is but the type of all bad habits; a little more desperate, perhaps, because it has worked itself into every fibre of the body, and made its gratification to be clamored for by every organ and function, every muscle, sense, and nerve; but all bad habits, in their place, exercise the same insane dominion. Sloth — is not the man ashamed of it? does he not make vows against it? does he not mourn at the ruin and disgrace it entails upon him? and yet he is slothful still. Ill-temper — does not the passionate mother, whose bursts of anger lead her to ill-treat the child that she loves, blush at her own shame, and condemn herself with bitterness and tears? and yet to-morrow the passion is her master again. Procrastination — with what keen anguish, with what abiding sense of degradation, with what remorse for friends neglected, duties omitted, precious opportunities of usefulness passed by, and occasions of honor and improvement lost forever, — with what compunction and self-condemnation, with what torment of unintermitting self-dissatisfaction, — does that inexplicable habit pursue its poor deluded victim! And yet remorse and shame, and a thousand injurious results, and the appeal even of sober principle, are vain. He still submits to his master, and will be wiser *to-morrow.* Other instances any one can add. And they suggest the fearful question, which almost staggers our hope as we reply to it — whether, in sober truth, a confirmed ill habit be not incurable, and whether virtue have any prospect of gaining in the conflict.

The best answer is found in the appeal to opposite facts. The worst habits in the most desperate cases, and under the most unpromising circumstances, have been corrected. The history of the Christian religion is filled with examples. It has shown its divine power in these triumphs, and proved, by the wonderful trophies of its grace, in the amazing conversions from sin which it has wrought, that however desperate may seem to be the struggle between principle and habit, yet the good is the stronger, and must prevail in the end, whenever it is faithfully and perseveringly supported.

But how much faith and what long perseverance it demands!

From these extreme cases, then, the Christian, who is seeking improvement, must take both a warning and encouragement — a *warning* that he examine his condition, and be fully acquainted with every circumstance in his modes of life which threatens this ruinous ascendency over his principle; and an *encouragement* that, if he detect any which is interwoven with his whole being, so that to part with it is like parting with a right hand or right eye, he yet *is able to do it*, and to enjoy the happiness of deliverance.

He is especially to learn the great duty of seeing to it, from the first, that all his personal and social habits, his disposition of time, the order of his affairs, the customs of his daily life and business, be such as to facilitate his virtuous purposes, — such as to make devotion and religion easy to him, — such as to make holy thoughts and benevolent actions always in place, never incongruous, never irksome, because evidently *in the way* of other affairs. By this method, he should give to goodness the fairest chance of obtaining a complete ascendency over him. Principle, finding all the habits of life and mind congenial, would thrive, and strengthen, and assume the complete mastery.

To make this yet the more sure, let him take pains directly to aid and encourage his principle; not only by bringing it forward and making it active on great emergencies, but by allowing it, nay, calling on it, to exert itself constantly; giving it small tasks; cheering it by the pleasure of small triumphs; and, in a word, by making even those lesser offices of duty and kindness, — which other men do of course, and without thinking, — by making even them matters of principle, — turning them into thoughtful acts of religious obedience, doing them because they are consonant to faith, and are suitable to a spiritual and holy nature — whether he eats or drinks, or whatever he does, doing all to the glory of God, as to the Lord, and not to men. In this way, the full power of habit and all its noblest energies may be enlisted on the side of his improvement. Because, principle being often called into action, and being made the supreme deciding authority, more frequently than any thing else, the habit of acting from principle will become stronger than any other habit; will overcome, suppress, exclude every hostile habit: the opposition between principle and habit, which once so palsied the purpose and neutralized the efforts of virtue, will have ceased: and the forces once antagonistic having become united in the alliance of truth, having become in fact *one*, there can be no longer any serious impediment to the onward progress of the soul. *Being made free from sin, ye will become servants to God, and have your fruit unto holiness.*

CHAPTER VI.

MAXIMS ON WHICH THE EXPECTATION OF RELIGIOUS PROGRESS IS TO BE BUILT.

Let us suppose that the low views and the erroneous principles on which the Christian life is too frequently made to proceed are set aside. We next go on to state the maxims on which the expectation of Christian progress must be built.

And, first of all, it is evident that *there must be a beginning*. There is no such thing as setting out in the midst. There is a first step in every journey; there is the commencement of life in every germ. The religious life of the soul can form no exception: it must have a first step, a commencement. Define it as you please, — let it be the act of the human reason alone, — let it be the moral character as exhibited in daily life, — let it have no authority or guide but the individual judgment and will; still there must be a beginning somewhere, for the simple reason that the individual who exercises the judgment and will has a beginning; so that no one, by adopting a low idea of the nature of the religious life, can thereby escape the obligation to ascertain whether he have started on the true career, nor assume that he came into it as a matter of course when he came into the world. For into what did he then come? Into those very habits of decent living which, in his view, are the Christian life? Surely not. Those habits were formed at a time when he had power to form the opposite habits; when he had the opportunity to decide for himself which he would adopt; and when, from some motive or other, he did adopt the better rather than the worse. If he claims that these should satisfy his conscience, then he must be able to show that he adopted them of good intention, that he formed the purpose to possess and maintain this character. Either he formed the purpose, or he did not form it: if he never formed the purpose, but is what he is by pure accident, then, of course, he will not pretend to any more *virtue*, than if, by a similar accident, he had become any other character; and, on the other hand, if he formed the purpose and pursued it by resolute forethought and plan, then he made a beginning. Therefore, nothing can be more absurd than the idea so commonly and unthinkingly held by men, that they are in the midst of their religious progress, when they never formed a distinct intention of pursuing it, and cannot prove that they ever laid an express plan in relation to it.

Now, if this be true in regard to that low idea of the Christian life just referred to, how much more is it true of that correct and elevated idea which rises beyond the decencies of external morals, to the spiritual purity of the affections, companionship with Christ, and a universal holiness. This absolute and express devotion to things invisible and eternal, this perpetual and supreme reference to the spiritual, is not a state of mind which grows up spontaneously, which starts to being of itself, out of the incumbrances and occupations of this visible state; — it must be the result of effort, the effect of design. No man can have thus gained the mastery over the sensible present without having intended it and labored for it: he could not *do this* without fixing a mark on that era of his life; without being able to go back and say that *then* he made a beginning; not perhaps at such a day or hour, or even absolutely such a year; but certainly that at such a period of life he took a decided stand, and, by some process of mind more or less protracted, came to the express understanding with himself that he was bound by religious obligations.

This is the first element in the religious life — this settled purpose of soul, this distinct, acknowledged, cherished intention and plan to live for heaven. He that cannot convict himself of having deliberately formed such a purpose, who is not conscious of having meditated and acted upon such a plan, talks idly when he asserts that he is in the midst of a Christian course. He deceives himself. He wants the first element of the religious life.

Next to this purpose, religious progress demands *effort*. The purpose must not die in inaction; it must not, as, alas! is too frequently the case, waste itself in reverie and musing. That dreamy state of the mind, which loves to dwell in contemplation, — to sit with the eyes half closed and gaze on the visions of glory which the fancy brings before it, — to think of the admirable things that may be done, and the grand designs which it would be delightful to accomplish, — is an unprofitable state, and does little to advance the character. It is likely to enervate rather than to improve it. No purpose is of any value which does not ripen into action; and the ever-present purpose of Christian progress is nought, unless accompanied by ever-active effort.

Inaction is the death of all virtue, the palsy of the character. It accounts satisfactorily for the backwardness and meanness of Christian men in Christian attainments. One might almost fancy, from the sluggishness with which men hold their faith, that, in adopting the gospel as their hope and rule, they had simply placed themselves on board some convenient vessel sent for their deliverance, and now were quietly to float down the gentle stream to the great city of their rest; instead of which, all experience and all revelation teach them, that they are embarked on a wide and perilous ocean, where they must watch and toil, and where they can make no progress except they make effort.

Our infatuation on this point is dreadful. Nothing else comes without labor and perseverance. Learning, accomplishments, distinction, wealth, — they are all earned; and no man who desires them hesitates to pay for them the full price, enormous as it sometimes is, at which alone they can be possessed. But that greatest and highest attainment, a perfect human character, is to come of itself. The calm peace of self-government, — the holy luxury of heavenly-mindedness — the lofty and complacent dignity of spiritualized affections — the honor of being like God, and glory of entering with Jesus Christ into immortal purity and love, — this we expect to obtain by wishing: this vast acquisition, this unlimited and illimitable boon, we look at, we admire, we long for, we do not doubt we shall possess; and yet we make for it nothing like the effort which we make to get bread for our children and ornaments to our houses.

No wonder, then, that the Christian community improves so slowly. No wonder that exemplary patterns of Christian attainment are so rare. No wonder that, instead of seeing all around us those men of the beatitudes, those partakers of the divine nature, those illustrious imitators of God, of whom the New Testament speaks, and whom Christ meant to fashion as his peculiar people, we are compelled to mourn over inconsistency and frailty — compelled to hide a multitude of sins in our good men with the mantle of a wide charity — compelled to extenuate and apologize for our own and our brethren's faults, on the score of that human imperfection, which it is our shame that we have not long ago surmounted and repressed. No wonder that, in this laxness of exertion toward Christian perfection, the world still waits to comprehend the meaning of that description which speaks of a "royal priesthood," "sons of God," "perfect men in Christ Jesus." For where are they? Here and there one, just to satisfy us that the Word of God describes no impossibility — just enough to cast unspeakable reproach and shame on the indolence of the backward multitude of believers,

— backward, because they make no true effort to go forward.

But it is not this listlessness and inaction alone, to which we are to look as the cause of this imperfect measure of Christian attainment amongst us; — much is to be imputed also to *a certain vagueness in respect to the nature and order of Christian progress.* Men do not distinctly perceive what it is, nor how it should proceed. The same inaccurate and cloudy notions already adverted to, which persuade them that they are in the successful prosecution of a work they have never expressly begun, nor formed any express purpose of doing, lead them also to believe that it will be, by-and-by, successfully completed in some general way; but they have not described to themselves in what way it is to be. They indistinctly see they must go forward; but they have no clear, accurate idea of the path, and no idea whatever of the stages by which they are to proceed. In a word, their notion of the whole subject is general and confused, amounting to nothing more than that they are to be improving themselves and advancing toward heaven; that they are to grow better as they grow older; — but as to analyzing this idea, and reaching an actual understanding of the several points in regard to which they are to grow better, — this is foreign from their thought; and no wonder that this vagueness of purpose keeps them stationary.

The next point, therefore, to be considered is, that *religious progress is to be made by stages.* It is not merely proceeding, but proceeding from one point to another. It is not merely becoming better, but becoming better first in one respect and then in another.

All progress is from stage to stage. In the processes of nature it is so; — first the blade, then the ear, then the full corn in the ear; — a continued growth, but arriving at and passing certain *epochs* or *periods* as it proceeds. So in the growth of the human frame, and of the human mind; so in the advancement of society and knowledge. No science can be taught, no art can be learned, except in passing from step to step; one portion must be acquired first as a preparation for another, and the third can be reached only through the full comprehension of the second.

Why should religious knowledge and Christian character be exceptions? Why should we not expect in their pursuit also to find natural steps of advancement, which invite us to aim at one attainment in the first place, and to make that a stepping-stone for the next? And if our religious progress were divided out for us into portions, would not its accomplishment be more certain and more satisfactory?

It may not be easy — indeed, it is very difficult — to state distinctly and with philosophical exactness the successive stages of the religious progress; and for this reason, among others, that they cannot be precisely the same to all men. Even the author of that celebrated description of the Christian life which depicts the Pilgrim's Progress, though of a class of believers who have gone as far as any in making Christian experience of the same undeviating type in all individuals — has yet found it necessary to allow great varieties in the several histories which he framed. Greater varieties still will be allowed by most persons who consider carefully the infinite diversities which exist in the natural tempers and dispositions of men, and the circumstances of education, society, business, companions, forms of life, &c. in which men are placed. It is inevitable that, under this state of things, no minute account can be given of the stages of Christian progress which will precisely apply to all persons. We can state nothing more than a few general principles, of whose varying application every man must judge for himself.

Thus we may say, first, this culture of character which you have undertaken is a vast and complicated thing: it is not one thing, but many; and it demands equal watchfulness and effort in many directions, as to the thoughts, the passions, the words the actions. It demands right affections toward all objects that concern you in this world, and in the invisible world; the proper balance of the affections; the due adjustment of the habits with the principle; the true combination of freedom and restraint, of contemplation with action, of firmness with gentleness. It demands knowledge, self-restraint, watchfulness, and action, in so many directions, on so many subjects, and so unintermittingly, that to undertake the whole at once, to assume the equal charge of all, and attempt their faithful regulation at the same moment, is a task that might well seem desperate. The work must be divided and classified; the field must be separated into portions; special attention must be first bestowed on this, and then on that, and the huge labor be facilitated by partition, the long journey accomplished by stages.

Then, secondly, as respects the precise order in which the several objects shall be taken up and accomplished, it is clear that the first care should be to establish the dominion of some great leading principle in the soul, some one master authority, to whose pervading influence all shall submit, and from whose absolute word there shall be no appeal. This will be to lay the foundation of the character steadfast and strong, and to further and facilitate the unity and compactness of the whole structure. And the Creator has provided for this in the very constitution he has framed, by making conscience the supreme power, and ordaining that every faculty and disposition shall bow to its sway. *To assure to conscience its rightful sovereignty* is, therefore, the first object; to this one great end the attention should be directed and the chief effort made, because, until conscience sits monarch in the soul, all effort after permanent moral advancement must be vain; and afterward none can be lost; and in the mean time, while this is going on, much discipline of the heart and the life will be unconsciously accomplished which otherwise might demand serious labor. Let the vigor of the soul, then, be concentrated to the accomplishment of this result, rather than dissipated and enfeebled in the attempt to perform several acts of inferior moment.

Having made some progress in this great work, there is another distinct object which may in the same way command the special attention of the soul, and be made matter of studious and almost exclusive consideration — the *predominant affection*, namely. This is of not inferior consequence to that just mentioned. That to which the heart is devoted decides the character; and if the character is matter of solicitude, especially is it matter of solicitude to decide what shall be mistress of the heart. Here the case is plain. LOVE is the first and second thing; love is the fulfilling of the law; he that dwells in love dwells in God. This is the principle that must sway the affections: when it does, the law will be fulfilled, and the soul will dwell with God, without any minute and painful toiling after the petty details of duty. Let this, then, be a distinct study, — the separate and express aim, — until the characteristics of divine love are impressed deeply on the heart, and all meaner affections recognize and bow to its dominion.

Another distinct object must be, to gain *an ever-wakeful consciousness of the divine presence.* The good child must learn to feel the Father's presence, must never lose sight of his eye; and it is essential to spiritual growth that the spirit human should be always aware of its contact with the Spirit divine. This is to be learned. This must become a habit. And it can only be by making it a subject of distinct study and effort; so that the soul, which the officious senses would restrict to this visible scene of things, may be able to struggle away from them, and look alway at the things which are unseen and eternal.

Let these suffice for specimens of what is intended by stages in the religious progress. I trust I have said enough to exhibit my meaning clearly. The doctrine I would inculcate is, that, instead of proposing to ourselves, in general terms, the vast and vague purpose of becoming religious, we should parcel out our duty into its natural departments, and make each the object of separate discipline, until we have become in some measure adepts in it, and then attend in the same way to another. Of course, this method cannot be pursued to the letter; no one can exclusively cultivate his conscience, and have no care of his affections; nor cherish the thought of God, and yet neglect his conscience. On the contrary, attention to either of these objects greatly tends to fix attention on the other two; but unquestionably the greatest proficiency in regard to each and to all would be achieved by an effort specially directed to one at a time.

This general principle might be illustrated

and explained to a much greater extent; but enough has been said to render it intelligible, and show its application. One thing at a time, though a rule impossible to be literally adhered to, is yet, as far as it may be observed, as wise in the progress of the religious character as in any other important affair.

END.

www.ingramcontent.com/pod-product-compliance
Lightning Source LLC
LaVergne TN
LVHW010231110826
845151LV00004B/1256

* 9 7 8 1 4 2 5 5 2 4 9 5 1 *